Into the Rabbit Hole

The Final Type

Book 6

Books by Micah T. Dank

Into the Rabbit Hole *series*

Book 1: Beneath the Veil

Book 2: The Sacred Stones

Book 3: The Secret Weapon

Book 4: Pangaeas Pandemic

Book 5: The Hidden Archives

Book 6: The Final Type

Coming Soon!

Book 7: The Unbegun

Into the Rabbit Hole

The Final Type

Book 6

Micah T. Dank

SPEAKING VOLUMES, LLC
NAPLES, FLORIDA
2021

The Final Type

ISBN 978-64540-527-6

This book is dedicated to Joanie who saved my life right before I started writing and Aunt Bonnie and her 7 kids, Gabriella, Stormy, Chloe, Garrett, Georgie, Flashy, and Bozo

Religion is regarded by the common people as true, by the wise as false, and by the rulers as useful—Seneca

Chapter One

Christmas was illegal in the US until 1836 as it was considered an ancient pagan holiday.

"What the hell do you mean the Pindar?" I asked the smokey gentleman still standing in our living room.

"Things aren't what they seem anymore. There is an internal power struggle among the elite. The balance of power that has been going on for thousands of years and the pecking order is about to undergo a serious change," the man said as he stubbed his cigarette and pulled out a cigar from his pocket. He bit the head off and spit it into a cup, looked us over with a wide smile full of tobacco in his teeth and lit it up.

"Do you think you could maybe not do that in our house?" Hannah asked.

"Why not? This is a great day for us. Your team is together, stronger than ever, and will help us set things back to the way they were," the man said.

"The way they were was not helping civilization and society. What makes you think I have a bit of interest in helping you? I don't even know your name," I said.

The man sighed, took a deep breath of the cigar and slowly blew it out towards the ceiling fan.

"These bombs that are hidden, nobody can figure out where they are. The plan is to destroy something so precious to us, so vital to our survival, that once it's done, will leave us helpless. Then the real plan for extermination begins," the man said, still not revealing his name.

"Even if we wanted to help," Josh began, "Where and how are we supposed to start?" he asked.

The man smiled again, big, like Denzel Washington in Training Day. "There is going to be a giant astrological event that will happen in the future. Nobody knows when or what. That's the way things go around here. It's always on a space clock. Once the event happens, they will hold the annual meeting at the Big Heaven Room. You will need to infiltrate it, find the Pindar and find out what she knows," the man said.

"Infiltrate the Big Heaven Room?" I asked. A creep shuddered up my spine and my balls dropped.

"Precisely," the man said.

"How do we know what the event will be?" I asked.

"Trust me, you'll hear about it. It might be subtle. Remember when 9-11 happened and they told us that only one dog died. Do you remember its name?" He asked me.

I shook my head.

"It was Sirius. Now do you think that was a metaphor or by accident?" He continued.

"Actually, wait. I think I knew about that. So, you mean it might not be an astrological event, just something astrological in general?" I asked.

"Truthfully I have no idea. I must leave now," the man said as he smashed his cigar into the overflowing cup of water and handed it to Rosette. He made his way down the stairs, careful not to trip the wire and left. He never even gave us his name.

We all sat down on our couch together collectively. Truthfully, the medicine I was on made it easier for me to think, I didn't have such a rush of voices in my head or a crazy stream of consciousness. Everything seemed flattened a bit. I still had my wit and charm, that didn't change, but overall, I can't believe it took me this long to figure out something was wrong with me.

"All right, so does anyone have any ideas?" Jackson asked.

We all shook our heads.

"Come on guys, we've got to figure something out," he said.

"I am just so seriously sick and tired of having to fix everyone's problems. Why can't we just be normal people?" I asked.

"Without you guys, without us, things would have gone horrible a long time ago," Josh said.

"Yeah, and what did he mean your knowledge of occult?" Jean asked him.

"Believe me guys, there's a ton of things in my head that I wish wasn't. But I have no idea what he meant," Josh said.

We sat there and turned on Blur Slanders. He was talking about how Christmas used to be illegal in Massachusetts from 1681-1870. Apparently, people had been drinking too much as well as crossdressing. I sat up for a minute to turn the TV off, until I sat up and had a realization. This guy Blur had infiltrated the Big Heaven Room a few years ago and took a video camera into it. He filmed some of the secret ceremonies there. If there was somebody that we needed to talk to about this, it was him. It would have to wait though, as we didn't know what exactly we were looking for. Everything for the near future was going to be suspect. My thoughts were interrupted.

"How are you feeling Graham?" Jackson asked.

"I'm doing ok. The problem isn't the medicine, it's the cost," I said.

"What do you mean?" He asked.

"What I mean is that each company gets something like 7 years a patent on a medication in order to make back all the money on R&D and then it should be able to go generic. One of my medications Latuda, without insurance is about $2000 a month. It's been more than 7 years and still no generic has come out. I'm going to run out of my Bar Mitzvah money paying for this thing unless I get these royalties from the Studio soon," I said.

"Right, about that. When are they filming?" Rosette asked.

"In about a month. I'm also playing the bartender in a scene, so hopefully the world doesn't go tits up before then," I finished.

"Alright guys, there's nothing more that we can do today, we just have to wait. We should all get going," Jackson said.

"Right," Jean said.

Just then it had occurred to me. The message from the Pleiadeans. The one that Dr. Cortese played for me. Their response!

"Guys, remember the message I received from Dr. Cortese about the Pleiadeans answer to my question?" I asked hopefully thinking that somebody would remember.

"Yeah, you never told us what it was, we figured it was personal and never bugged you for it. Why? What did they say?" Hannah asked.

"They said for there to be true peace we were going to have save the Starseeds. They said that we would be put in an impossible situation, and that not all of us were going to make it out alive, but if we succeed, our story would be world known and there would be a global armistice while we cleared out the powers that be," I said.

"What do they mean the Starseeds?" Rosette asked.

"Honestly I have no idea. Starseeds are a new generation of people, souls sent to Earth in this new day and age or eon in Aquarius that will help bring peace to the world. Much like the Indigo Children. They don't feel they originated on this earth, that their souls come from far away. They're very in tune with themselves. You hear about the kids in Tibet, over a million gathered together to meditate at the same time. It's been proven that when a large group of monks came to DC a while back and meditated together, the crime rate dropped a significant portion in DC for the weekend. These people don't have a religion, don't have a savior, are only here for our betterment. But I don't know how we're supposed to save all the Starseeds though. Also, they were adamant that we're all not going to make it to the end of this," I said.

"Well, don't read into it right now, Graham, there's literally nothing we can do as of now," Larisa said.

I was beginning to wonder when Larisa would join this conversation.

"Basically, once we get this magical sign that they're waiting on, I need to talk to Blur," I said.

"Makes sense," Jackson said.

"Do you have to baby?" Hannah asked.

"As much as he's crazy, he's the only one that's been in there and got out alive," I said.

"All right, so we're going home. Keep us posted." Jean said as everyone left.

I went back into our master bedroom and sat down at the desk. I opened my computer and started writing notes for the series until my eyes couldn't take it anymore, and I passed out. Hannah dragged me to the bed half asleep and took my shoes off for me. As usual with us, we were about to get the wakeup call of our lives at the strangest time.

The world is passing through troubling times. The young people of today think of nothing but themselves. They have no reverence for parents or old age. They are impatient of all restraint. They talk as if they know everything, and what passes for wisdom with us is foolishness with them. As for the girls, they are forward, immodest and unladylike in speech, behavior and dress—Peter the Hermit (A thousand years ago)

Chapter Two

One Month Later

Sanity is judged by society's collective acceptance of a delusion. If you aren't someone the Church would have killed 400 years ago, are you even living? Well, I'm someone that the Church is trying to kill NOW. The only reason I've been able to make it this far is because there is a small fraction of the elite that is trying to help me. I would have been dead many times over the past few years. As Salman Rushdie said, "Perhaps the story you finish is never the one you begin." If he could survive the threats of death from the religious, I sure as hell can.

There's something called claircognizance, which is when information comes to your mind suddenly without logic, without prior knowing, without reasons, or even memory. It is just a certain and strong knowing. There is no room for doubt, it just is what it is. That is how I've been able to figure out these Biblical riddles as it pairs with astrology. I just understand the language and yes, it does speak to me. I think, therefore I am used to be the only thing I could know for certain, but since this all began with the letter from my brother, I know now that EVERYTHING is just hidden astrology/astrotheology and astronomy. I will get to a few further examples in a moment.

Did you know that there is a Martian calendar out already? It's been created for when we terraform the planet within the next 50 years if Elon Musk has his way. It's 24 months of 28 days each, and each is named after a Latin and Sanskrit constellation. Think about that for a second. The first thing we do when we attempt to normalize the idea of living on another planet is to create its calendar and name it after constellations.

The Grolier Codex is the oldest book written in the American Continent that has been found, and it's a Mayan guide to Astronomy.

The Voynich Manuscript, long thought to be written by the language of the aliens, for hundreds of years nobody could figure it out. Eventually someone did and it turned out to be at least in part, revolving around Astrology.

The Antykythera Mechanism, one of the greatest secrets on Earth, once decoded was discovered to be an extremely early computer that mapped out the skies. Another Astrology/Astronomy device that came to light.

Gobekli Tepe, is a site from 11000 years ago. On the stones are carved mysterious symbols, animals in fact. These turned out to be astronomical symbols. Amongst other things, Gobekli Tepe was an observatory for monitoring the night sky. Chantal Jeguez-Wolkiewiez found that the constellations match up with the cave paintings in Lascaux at that time frame. She figured out that by superimposing the night sky as seen at that time frame, tens of thousands of years ago, the drawings match up to the constellations.

Starting to see the picture? It's not only that. There are so many more examples within the Bible that deal directly with Astrology. It permeates in pop culture today as well.

The Bull and the Bear markets at Wall Street in New York City get their name they say because the bull goes horns to the sky to attack, which indicates a good market, and the bear 'paws down' to attack, indicating a recession of sorts. What people don't know is that the Bull is in Taurus, where the Sun is climbing 1 degree a day until it hits June 21st, and then its decreasing by the time it hits the Bear, or Ursa Minor (which is in Leo). I may have mentioned this before, but why does the stock market always crash horribly during Libra?

Going back to the Bible we can see the story of Jonah and the Whale. The story goes that Jonah was trying to divert from his duty and God sent a storm to him, he was swallowed by a fish, repented and was released. However, Astrologically it tells a different story. The Constellation Cetus is a constellation that borders both Aquarius and Pisces. Cetus means Whale or 'Great Fish'. Jonah is represented by the sign of the Man, Aquarius, and the Fish is by Pisces. This is another story about being swallowed up and being dead for 3 days, that magical time frame, before being released.

♍ This is the glyph for Virgo. It is an M with a standing up Pisces attached to it, almost as if the M is cradling a baby. Which makes sense, Pisces and Virgo are opposing signs and share energies. However, in Astrotheology it's different. You have the Virgin Mary, Adonis's mother Myrra, Buddhas mother Maya, Horus' mother IsisMeri. All the mother's names start with an M. Especially in Christianity this is prevalent because the New Testament was written during the time of Pisces. But it doesn't stop there. In the Book of Micah, he predicts that from Bethlehem a savior will come. Well, that would make sense if you understood Hebrew. Bethlehem is two Hebrew words combined, Bet and Lehem. The two words translate to House and Bread. The House of Bread. So from the House of Bread (The Virgin holding the wheat stalk) a savior would be born. A savior, born to a virgin.

In the same way that Pisces is standing up in the Virgo glyph, if you were to raise the DMT molecule which is responsible for our dreaming and visiting other dimensions, straight up, it's almost the spitting image to Orion. As above, so below indeed.

Lastly, the Bible wasn't completely edited until the King James Bible came out in 1611. However, it did have a little help from a well-known author. William Shakespeare left his signature within the Bible, and it has to do with the number 46. Shakespeare was 46 years old in 1611 when the Bible came out. Psalm 46, if you count the 46th word from the top you get Shake (The Earth doth shake), and the 46th from the bottom is spear (God cutteth forth a spear).

More and more I'm being convinced that religious people are drawn to their holy texts because they are absolutely terrified about death. Well, religion solves that problem for them. You don't need a holy text to show you how to live a good life, you have a brain that tells you right from wrong. At the same time, I find that all the atheists out there are more than likely atheists, not because the idea of a God isn't possible, but because they despise with what the religious people say God is and what it wants. Just be careful when you get to the point in your life where you think you know the answers and that you are right. The smartest people in history all knew that they didn't know anything from the cradle to the grave. Both religious and atheists profess the Hegelian Dialectic. First create the problem, then sell the solution. Lastly, as JP Morgan famously said, 'Millionaires don't use Astrology, Billionaires do.' Do what you will with this. Call me a crazy conspiracy theorist, call me a genius. At the end of the day, what I have, what my friends and I have seen so far seems to fall directly in line with this.

I saved it and closed my laptop. Just then Hannah walked into the room.

"You've been up since 5am. You feeling ok?" She asked.

"Yeah, it's fine, I was just finishing up my epilogue on the series as requested," I said.

"You know critics and bloggers are going to say that your books are too short." She giggled.

"Screw them. They're as long as they're supposed to be. Enough to get our stories across," I said.

"Well, come back to bed baby, you have a busy day tomorrow. We're all coming with you to the Fours to get a few drinks and watch you film your scene," she said.

"Yeah, that's a good point, I don't have to be there until 6 anyway." I said as I put my laptop away and took out the flash drive and put it in my jeans pocket. Never leave home without it.

I started to doze off, thinking about all the things I had just written about. Wondering how it would be taken by the masses. What new people I would piss off. Hope that it would make its way to the elites that have had my back this whole time. What I didn't know at the time of me passing out was that the 'event' was going to interrupt my filming.

Chapter Three

We woke up around noon after the best night's sleep I've had in my life. I felt refreshed and full of life. My medicine was really starting to work. Things couldn't be going better for me. I hadn't thought about having a drink in a while now. We showered and got dressed for the day. Everyone met at our house around 2. We were on our way to the Fours to make history.

We got to the Fours around 2:30 as the film crew was setting up. Don Harrow, the director, noticed me immediately and made his way to me.

"Hey Graham, it's so good to finally meet you. I'm Don," he said.

"Hi Don, I know who you are, you're an unbelievable storyteller," I said.

"Well thank you. However, it's you that's the great storyteller. We're just going over lighting and sound right now. The actor who's playing you is Fez Anchor, I'm sure you've heard of him. He's going to be coming in a little bit. For now, we are in an active bar, why don't you and your friends saunter up there and get something to drink and sit at one of the tables in the back room," Don said.

"You got it, Don. Thank you so much," I said.

We made our way to the bar and tried to get the bartenders attention. Finally, after a long moment she turned around.

"Hi Graham, what can I get you guys?" She said.

It took me a minute to realize who she was, but this was Chrissie Mayr. She was a comedian/actor that was starting to make a name for herself in New York. I've seen some of her stuff in the Aquastream comedy hour. She was unmistakable. Fire red hair, slim, petite and very loud and hysterical.

"What are you doing here Chrissie?" I asked.

"Oh, I landed the role of bartender 2 in your movie Graham, looks like we'll be twerking the bar together. What can I get you guys while I'm back here?" She asked.

"Let's go with two towers of Bud light," I said.

"No problem, I'll bring them over to you when they're ready. See you soon," she said.

We walked back to one of the tables and put our jackets down when I noticed someone familiar setting up audio on the stage. They somehow brought Jake Incao in for some background scene. Truth is, I hadn't read the script, only my lines, I had no idea they would have my favorite musician in here. I made my way up to him.

"How's it going buddy?" I asked.

"This is big for me Graham. Thank you so much for writing me into your stories. This could be the big break I've been waiting for," Jake said.

"So, what are you doing back here?" I asked.

"Basically, soft background music and playing for a bunch of extras I'm assuming," he said.

"That's awesome. Hey, make sure you play Let's Talk or Still Forever. Those are my two favorite songs from you," I said.

"You got it. Thank you again for everything buddy. It's really changed my life." Jake said as he started tuning his guitar and turned around from me.

I made my way back to the table. The two towers were waiting there, and everyone already poured themselves a glass. My diet coke was waiting for me. I sat down with my friends with a big smile on my face.

"So what do you think guys. I'm starting a premium Aquastream chatroom called the 'Illuminaughty' where I talk to conspiracy theories, and they pay me to see my tits!" Rosette squealed.

"I don't know about that Rose." I said as I laughed.

We sat around and bullshat for about half an hour, everyone pounding their drinks. Then when the buzzes hit them, things got really interesting.

"So what is Mercury Retrograde Graham, and why are people so wacky around it?" Larisa asked.

"So basically, Mercury has a smaller orbit around the Sun. When it passes Earth in its smaller orbit which is 3 times a year, it appears that Mercury is moving backward. It's an illusion. Honestly, I don't think it has an effect on anyone the way people go nuts. Honestly, I think the Moon controlling the tide has much bigger control over us, more so women," I said.

Larisa pretended to stroke her beard and furrowed her eyebrows.

"So what you're saying is, if you've had sex with every Zodiac sign, that would make you an ASStrologer?" She said.

I choked on my Diet Coke. I was not ready for this conversation.

"I guess you could say that Larisa." I said, looking over at Jean. He had his head in his hands as he clearly knew how the girls were about to get.

"Well, ASStrologer or not, I'm definitely a Taurus," Rosette said.

"Me too," Jackson replied.

"No you're not, you're a Scorpio," Rosette said.

"That's not true. I'm a Taurus because I tore that ass up this morning!" Jackson replied.

I almost dropped my drink.

"Oh, suck my cliTAURUS Rider," Rosette said

"I'm sorry, did the Physicist just make an Astrology joke? Maybe we can end up friends after all Jax," I said.

He looked at me and smiled.

"I want in on that channel girl." Larisa turned to Rosette.

Rosette giggled.

"Double sided Dildo. The Chinese finger trap of lipstick lesbians," I said.

"I would like to buy all the subscriptions so nobody can see it but me," Jean said.

"Sorry baby, but it's too much pork for just one fork," Larisa said.

"Yeah, Sorry Solex, but it's too much poon for one little spoon," Rosette said.

"It's too much knife for one wife!" Jean shouted and smirked.

Everyone put their drinks down.

"See Jean, this is why we can't have nice things," Jackson said.

"Yeah dude, what the hell, you took it too far," Rosette said.

"Are you guys being serious right now?" Jean asked as he scanned the table.

We all kept it together as long as we could and then burst out laughing. Jean's face had a sigh of relief over it.

"I'm going to replace your birth control with MDMA when I get home." I said to Hannah.

"You and Jackson will both be sleeping on the couch together." She laughed.

"I'm cool with that bro. A little Headdie Mercury never hurt nobody," he said.

Josh laughed for the first time today. I was wondering what was going on in his mind up until now.

"That's not fair Hannah. You can't do that to me. Remember on our wedding night, when I carried you through the threshold and brought you upstairs and deflowered you?" I asked.

"Me a virgin. Yeah OK." She laughed.

"It's true!" I said.

"Actually, yeah it is. He had the Vagi-check," she said.

"What the hell is the Vagi-check? Rosette asked.

"It's this app that came out after that whole debacle with TI and his daughter getting checked to make sure she was still a virgin. Someone came out with an app that checks the hyman," I said.

Rosette's eyes got big real quick.

"I've been having sex workouts too!" Jean interjected.

"Jean, regardless of what you think, masturbation is not considered cardio," I said.

Everybody laughed.

"Well how come my fitbit goes ape when I do it then starboy," Jean said.

Everybody laughed.

Calling me a starboy reminded me of that quote about saving the Starseeds. For the last 20 minutes of us being around, I hadn't thought that something was going to happen soon. I felt a knot in my stomach. Usually, I'd pound a drink or 12 at this point, but instead I went in my jacket pocket, popped open my bottle of Seroquel and popped a 25mg pill.

"You OK baby?" Hannah asked as she looked over worried at me.

"I'll be fine lovebug," I said.

"I haven't heard any new Astrology from you in over a week. Are you sure you're OK?" Jackson asked me.

"You mean besides the retrograde conversation we just had?" I asked.

"Exactly," he said.

I looked over at him. "Don't make me go Ken Ham on your ass," I said.

He laughed.

"Which reminds me, I've been meaning to give this over to you." Jackson said as he pulled out a gift from his jacket and handed it to Rosette.

"Oooh, what is it?" She asked.

"Open it and see," Jackson said.

She opened the package and looked at it and smiled.

"Aw Rider, you named a Star after me as a birthday gift." She squealed.

He smiled. I burst out laughing.

"What's so funny Graham?" Jackson asked.

"It's not funny, it's sweet, it's just that." I couldn't finish my sentence I was laughing too much.

"What?" He asked.

"I mean you're a physicist. Haven't you ever heard of the Rosette Nebula?" I asked.

His eyes sank, when they came up to meet mine, he looked like a lost puppy.

"Wait, you mean there's a whole cluster in the sky named after me?" Rosette asked.

"Not after you, but yes. It's in the Monoceros region of the Milky Way," I said.

Rosette looked at Jackson and he smirked.

"If you look at it, it looks like a Rose," I said.

"Jackson, I want that Nebula named after me. The Rosette Rebel Nebula," she said.

"I'll see what I can do," he said.

"Girls always want so much from us guys," Jean said.

"Oh, don't be a misogynist," Hannah said.

"How can I be a misogynist. I'm engaged to a Dom," Jean said.

We all looked over at Larisa.

Larisa was mid drink on her beer. She put up her pointer finger indicating us to give her a minute. She finished her beer and started pouring another. The tanks were half empty at this point.

"You know Jean, I have told you in the past not to mention that in public. Now you must be punished." She said as she lifted her leg and put her foot on the bench we were sitting on. "Go on bad boy, lick my boot," she said.

His eyes got wide, and we all burst out laughing.

"Very hot Larisa. I give it a 90 on Rotten Tomatehoes.

She laughed.

"OK Graham, we're ready for you if you're ready for us. You just have to hit up hair and makeup first. Can we trim up your beard so you don't look like Rasputin?" Don said.

I smiled at him and turned to everyone and gave them a salute. I followed him to the chair. 25 minutes later I looked like the best version of myself.

"OK guys are we ready to roll?" Don asked.

I stepped behind the bar. Turned and smiled at Chrissie and turned back.

"Hi Graham, it's great to finally meet you."

I turned around and spun into my spitting image. This was Fez, and he was known in Hollywood as being a method actor. He had studied at the prestigious American Academy of Dramatic Arts in LA and was a breakout student. I guess he would be playing me.

"Where's the rest of the cast?" I asked him.

He smiled.

"This is the scene where you broke your sobriety. All you have to do is ask me what I want and make it for me." Fez said as he winked at me.

I could tell this kid had read all my books and done his homework. Also, he was right. I did rush here and pounded a bunch of drinks.

"OK everyone, we're rolling," Don said. "And action."

I came out from around the bar and faced Fez. I looked at him for a long moment.

"What can I get you?" I asked.

"CUT!" Don shouted. "Not enough going on here. Graham, the real Graham, need something to do with your hands, to look busy. Pick up that martini glass and the rag behind you and start drying it," Don said.

I nodded.

"All right we're rolling again. And action."

I came around the bend looking a bit overwhelmed while drying this already dry martini glass.

"What can I get you?" I said, looking around.

"Bartender please, fill my glass for me, with a Long Island Iced Tea. Also, let me get a shot of chilled Tito's Vodka." Fez said to me.

"Sure thing." I said as I turned around to make the drink. Just one problem, I have no idea how to mix drinks.

"Cut!" I yelled.

"What? This was going fine," Don said.

"I don't know how to bartend," I said.

"I'll make the drink for you sweet stuff. It'll be in a mixer behind you. Just chill the shot and hand it to him," Chrissie said.

Thank God for her right now.

"Alright everyone, let's get one for the record books." Don said as he waited a moment for Chrissie to basket weave a perfect Long Island Iced Tea. Knowing Fez, he would actually drink legit drinks, being all methody and such.

"Action," Don said.

I sauntered around the bend with a busy look on my face. I cleaned the martini glass and set it back with the others. I turned to Fez and smiled at him.

"What can I get you?" I asked.

"Bartender please, fill my glass for me, with a Long Island Iced Tea. Also, I'll take a shot of Tito's vodka chilled please," he said.

"You got it. You got a name for a tab?" I asked him.

"Graham. Graham Newsdon," Fez said.

It was surreal hearing that. I was trying very hard not to get overwhelmed.

I turned and got a sifter and poured some ice in it, then carefully measured a shot of vodka into it. Shook it up and poured it into a shot glass. Then I turned my back to him and got the drink that Chrissie made. I grabbed a tall glass and poured the contents into it and finished it off with a paper straw, because you know, environment.

"Hey Bartender, do you mind turning that T.V. up a little?" Fez asked me.

I turned to look for the remote and it was closer to Chrissie.

"Chrissie, toss me the remote." I improvised with an outstretched hand.

She turned and smiled and did exactly that.

I turned to put the volume up on the TV. This was supposed to be when the news reporter broke the conclave story. Instead, I looked at the TV.

We waited there for a minute, then Fez paid his tab and left.

“CUT!” Don said. “Graham, that was great. I think we caught everything,” he said.

“What about the TV though, it’s playing something else?” I asked.

“Naw, we’ll edit it out post prod. The important part is done. We’re going to wrap up here now, we’re finished for now.” Don said as he shook my hand. I gave him a salute and he walked off.

I walked outside and lit a cigarette. It had been a good few hours since my last one, and this one was starting to feel so good. I looked up at the sky and saw the Sun starting to set a little bit. Then something caught my eye at about 30 degrees to the left of the Sun. There was a bright flashing, pulsating light in the sky. It wasn’t a plane, and it was too bright out for it to be a star. I snubbed my cigarette and made my way back into the bar where everyone was gathered around the TV.

“Graham, you’re uh, going to want to see this,” Jackson said.

I came up to the very TV I was under. I didn’t notice it when I was mid scene, but the channel I put on was the News. They’re saying that there was a large discharge in the sky and people are still trying to figure out what it was. No planes have been reported missing. I opened my phone to check on the alternative media that I usually watch, and there were already articles up. What I read shook me. Betelgeuse had exploded and gone Supernova. The armpit of Orion was no more. This must have been the event that we have been waiting for. What sets it all off. I put Blur Slanders on my phone, and he wasn't covering it. He was talking about how about an hour ago the Big Heaven Room had decided to meet months early for their getaway. It didn't take a genius to realize that the two were connected. If we were going to infiltrate the Big Heaven Room and locate the Pindar, we were going to have to speak to the one person who successfully infiltrated it a few years back and lived to tell the tale. We were going to have to get Blur Slanders to talk to us once again.

I picked up the phone and called into his show. They bumped me up right to him. He had left his second Palau Towns to run the news while he took my call.

"What's up kid?" He asked.

"I need to talk to you about the Big Heaven Room. I need to infiltrate it," I said.

There was a silence on the other end of the line.

"I'm vacationing in New Hampshire at the end of the week. I'll swing by Boston and talk," he said.

"I appreciate that, where do you want to meet?" I asked.

"In public. Figure it out." He said as he gave me his personal phone number and hung up the phone.

We had two days to figure out the logistics of this and get our list of questions together. This wasn't going to be something easy, in fact it would prove to be one of the most insanely dangerous things we've ever done.

As long as we believe absurdities, we will commit atrocities—Voltaire

Chapter Four

Two days later

We woke up early and had breakfast. This was going to be that kind of day, so we wanted to fuel up. Blurs plane would be landing soon, and we needed to make our way to the Central Wharf. We packed food for the day and got in Jean's van. There wasn't much traffic on the road which was a shocker.

We got to the Central Wharf and went up to the Boston Duck Tours window. We paid for all the seats on the trip. We couldn't risk anybody hearing what we were talking about, and we certainly didn't want anybody needing any celebrity pictures of Blur. After about an hour and a half, Blur showed up.

"How's it going Graham, guys. It's great to see you. What kind of nonsense have you gotten yourselves into this time?" he asked.

Straight to the point with this guy.

"We're good. Listen, can we get on the boat and talk there?" I asked.

"Sure thing Graham," he said.

We boarded the boat, and it took off fifteen minutes later.

"So before we start, I need to know how you did it," Blur said.

"How I did what?" I asked.

"Not you, Larisa. How did you get that 2-million-dollar contract with Mayim Bank?" He asked.

Larisa's jaw dropped.

"How did you know about that?" She asked.

"I make it a point to know everything about everyone. It's what's kept me alive this far. Are you going to tell me?" he asked.

I turned to Larisa confused. She hadn't mentioned anything about this to me. I scanned the room to see if everyone had the same reaction. Only Jean seemed to smile.

"It's kind of a dumb story," she said.

"Still want to hear it," Blur replied.

"All right. So, a while back I had emailed the head of IT and asked if I broke into their system and shut down the ATMs if they would give me a contract to rebuild their security system. Eventually it was kicked up to the VP and he wrote back "Yes". They both mocked me because they didn't think it was possible. Anyway, I went to the big branch in Dorchester and studied it for weeks. I noticed that every Tuesday they would order pizza for everybody from Angelina's. So, I bought a pizza delivery outfit and hacked the pizzeria's phone system. I waited for their order. Finally it came, so I went into Angelina's and told them I was from Mayim and I was picking up the order today. They seemed to agree with me because, like clockwork, they used to receive an order from them every Tuesday, it was weird that they had not gotten a call yet. I paid for the pizzas and put them in my car. I drove over to the bank and went inside. I tipped my hat to the front desk and put the pizzas through the scanner. I went through the metal detector and had the whole TSA groping experience. I then took the pizzas up to the main room where all the hotshots were. On my way out, I stopped by the desk before going back through security and asked to use the bathroom. The lady at the desk pointed me to it. I went into the bathroom and went into one of the stalls. When the women left the restroom, I stood up on the toilet and punched a hole in the ceiling to remove one of the squares. Someone came back in, so I ducked back down in the stall. After she left, I climbed up into the AC Vent and put the square back up. It was about 2pm. I waited up in that vent until 8pm when everybody left for the day and the building locked, and security was put on. I was already through security, so when I came down and went out into the lobby, nobody was there. Because they believed in their security so much, they didn't have people patrolling. I walked towards the head of IT's room and the door was unlocked. I went over to his computer and turned it on, but there was a password on it. Usually, 90% of people leave their passwords on a sticky note by their desk, but this guy didn't. I ended up finding it in a jacket in his closet and logged in. I then planted a virus that disabled the ATM's and left the building. I then rang him up and told him what I did. That's when they offered me a 2-million-dollar deal to create their security," Larisa finished.

I stared at her and blinked.

"How long have you been sitting on this information?" I asked. The truth was, although Jean was loaded, I did find it a little strange that Larisa was basically cash cow sugar mama for us recently.

"I mean, it's only been a few weeks," Larisa said.

"That's a brilliant story. Tell me, when you were up in the vent for 6 hours, what did you do if you had to pee?" Blur asked.

"That's easy. I wore a diaper that day," Larisa said.

Again, a bunch of staring at her with our jaws dropped.

"Sorry guys, I haven't gotten around to telling you this until now. I was kind of playing it close to the chest," Larisa said.

"That's fine girl. Congrats," Rosette said.

"All right guys, so now that foreplay is out of the way, what am I doing here?" Blur asked.

The boat shook around. It was a rather windy day. "We need to break into the Big Heaven Room. Something big is going to happen," I said.

Blur took a deep breath and rubbed his head with his hands. "You guys know how difficult it is going to be to duplicate?" He asked.

I shook my head.

"To be able to go there you first have to understand what they even do there. It's a ceremony of all the rich and most powerful people in the country. They go there to decide eugenics. They get together and they drink and smoke and do drugs and decide what group they are going to eradicate next. Then they all go back to their countries and implement laws and manipulate the news in order to get what they have decided. You see, it's called the revelation of the method. David Wilcock talks about it a lot. The elites are bound by this rule that they HAVE TO tell you what they are doing. It's a law that they are bound by if they want to continue to operate. These people, they believe in the highest power of satanism and occult worship. But in the end, as the Bible says, Satan will lose the great war," Blur finished.

"Wait, back it up a few seconds. What do you mean drink and do drugs?" I asked.

Blur's eyes got wide.

"You have no idea. These aren't regular drinking and drugs. These people deal in adrenochrome," Blur said.

"What's adrenochrome?" Hannah asked.

"You didn't tell her, did you?" He said as he looked at Josh.

Josh shook his head.

"It's better that most people don't know. There is a drug that was first made popular by Hunter S. Thompson in his famous Vegas book and movie called adrenaline. Human adrenaline. The best way to get it and get high from it is to take a child and scare the ever-loving crap out of him/her. I mean, really terrify them so their fight or flight adrenaline kicks in," Blur said.

"Then what?" Rosette asked.

"Then, they cut the child open, drain their blood and pass it around and drink it. The high I'm told is out of this world," Blur said.

Rosette and Hannah gagged.

"Are you being serious right now?" Jean asked.

"You do remember that I was literally there, right? My videos I took didn't capture it, but that's what they do. The first night there is a giant sacrifice of a child. The elites stand around him or her, each with a knife while the child is tied to a table. A bucket is placed under him or her. Then, the ones that are up there take turns stabbing the child and draining his or her blood. The people who have the knives that participate are the next in line for supreme power in the world. Everybody that is somebody in the world has a secret like this on film that could destroy them. Some are pedophilia, necrophilia, some are adrenochrome ceremony," Blur finished.

"What happens next?" I asked.

"Basically, when they're all high, they find the cabin that they're staying in and go there. Prostitutes both male and female are brought into the room as well as any kind of drug you imagine. Usually a big orgy from there, but sometimes you can catch them one on one," Blur said.

"What about the Pindar?" Josh asked.

I flashed him an angry look. I didn't want that to come up yet.

"Wait, you guys are going after the Pindar?" Blur asked looking uncomfortable. "If that's the case, than just me talking to you has jeopardized my life. Why the hell didn't you tell me when you were on the phone with me earlier Graham?" Blur asked angrily.

"Please Blur, you're the only one that can help us. You have to tell us. Is she there?" I pleaded.

Blur looked over at us and his face started to calm down a little bit.

“If I have to up my security because of you, I’m going to be major league pissed off. Yes, the Pindar is usually there, but I’ve heard some rumblings,” he said.

“About what?” Jackson asked.

“That times are a changing and that she’s not the head honcho anymore. She’s just a face for the elites, like the Royal Family is for England. They’re just important in name and nostalgia,” Blur said.

“What’s the best way for us to approach this?” I asked.

“Well first of all, it’s held in California in Moontier. Now, Moontier has an airport there, but if you park your fancy private jet there, it will raise suspicion. Your best bet would be to fly to San Francisco and then rent a car. It’s only about an hour and 45 minutes away from the airport,” Blur said.

“Ok, noted. What else?” I asked.

“You have to understand that most of the people that handle things at the Big Heaven Room have degrees in Soteriology from sacred academies. It’s the study of salvation in religions. Second, most of them and especially the Pindar, they don’t talk like me and you. They speak in parables, quatrains, and famous occult phrases. I’m assuming that’s where Josh comes in to play with this,” Blur said.

"If it's adrenaline, can't they just take an oxidized epi pen to get the same high?" I asked.

"That might work for normies like me and you, but there is something primal about taking the life of a missing child and consuming their essence. It's not just blood too, it's semen as well. It's just a great place to be," Blur said.

"What else can we do?" I asked.

"Basically, you need your little girl genius over here to break into the compounds ring network so that you can be guided from the beginning of the woods, until you get all the people. You'll need to create a diversion to get them all out to their rooms and then search for the Pindar. You'll need to really know your gray man persona Graham if you're doing this. Also, shave your head. You'll be less, famous for lack of a better word. I hope you know I was going to do an internet show for my audience today since I'm out. Did you know that during the Cold War, the CIA thought of dropping XL condoms labeled 'medium' over the Soviet Union to make them feel like less than manly men?" He finished.

Rosette laughed.

"You know it's not just my videos. There are other ones from people at the ceremony year after year. It's on the internet, but you'll never be able to find it," Blur said.

"And why's that?" Jackson asked.

"Because they're buried on Mariana's web. Ask your physicist and computer nerd what that is," Blur said.

I turned to Jackson and Larisa.

"Mariana's web is accessed by using a network of quantum computers. Quantum computers allow particles to exist in two states simultaneously, which would make it impossible for hackers to hack. Jackson, you know all about quantum superposition in physics and how something can exist in multiple places at once. The way that computers are binary as 1's and 0's, in quanta, it can be BOTH one and zero at the same time," Larisa said.

"The problem is that these computers can only exist in a crazy impossible environment. You're talking super cooling, pressure and vacuum in miniscule amounts," Jackson said.

"I feel like you guys are gangbanging my brain right now," I said.

"Is this something that we can access?" Jean asked.

We all looked at him.

"Are you here with us in this conversation right now Jean?" Rosette asked.

"Never mind that now guys. You should also know that in the facility, there is a dark room, a leather room and a necrophilia room. Most of the people that frequent there are part of Uncle Sam's Snuff Factory. Which, I'm not getting into with you right now. Look, this is where I get out guys. I've given you all that I know. The truth is that only about two or three of you are going to be able to go in there in order to blend. The rest are going to have to hang back. Remember this if you remember anything. There are beings in the spiritual realms for whom anxiety and fear emanating from human beings offer welcome food. When humans have no anxiety and fear, then these creatures starve. People not yet sufficiently convinced of this statement could understand it to be meant comparatively only. But for those who are familiar with this phenomenon, it is a reality. If fear and anxiety radiate from people and they break out in panic, then these creatures find welcome nutrition and they become more and more powerful. These beings are hostile towards humanity. That was Rudolph Steiner. Thanks for the free ride Graham. Keep me posted." Blur said as he exited the boat which just returned to shore and walked off into the wild.

"Guys, we're going to have to go over a few things, I can't do this alone," Josh said.

"What do you mean do this alone?" I asked.

"I just don't know enough to guide you through this, even if you're wearing earpieces. I have to explain the different kind of people that we might encounter," Josh said.

"What do you mean encounter?" Larisa asked.

"There are a few different types of people. The first type are atheists who don't believe in God/Devil. They don't believe in anything. The second type are Christians who believe that Lucifer is Satan and is constantly fighting over your soul. Albeit Graham makes a strong case that Lucifer and Satan are neither real, nor are they the same, it is what it is. The third type are Satanists who don't believe in a real Satan. These are people who believe more closely to atheists that you have only one life and to basically as LaVey put it 'Don't be a dick' and satisfy the self. Here's where it gets dicey. The fourth type are Satanists who believe in a literal Satan and are out to destroy everything. Now you have to understand that most Satanists are the former, they believe in humanism. As Pacino as Satan said in the Devil's Advocate he's a humanist. Most of them try to be that." He paused for a moment. "Then there's the final type. The final type are the movers and shakers of the world. Politicians, elite Wall Street, high ranking church members, foreign councils. They all believe in a dark power, we'll call it Satan, Moloch, Beelzebub, Magog, what have you. They, as Blur said, routinely sacrifice people to it and video tape each other. To get to that level of elite fame or elite wealth, you have to have a secret that can take you down. That's why Epstein was murdered. He was ready to testify and bring down the entire child sacrifice/pedophilia operation. Whether it's pedophilia or animal sacrifice, or human sacrifice, you must be filmed doing one of them. These are the most dangerous types of people, the people that meet at the Big Heaven Room. If they find any of you out, they will never find your body. They are very fond of acid baths and making a smoothie out of you. Seriously, cadaver dogs wouldn't even pick up your scent. Unfortunately, we're going to need help from one of these groups if we're going to infiltrate. These people, they truly understand people like Anton LaVey, Aleister Crowley, Madame Blavatsky, Albert Pike, Eliphas Levi, Manly P. Hall, Nostradamus, et cetera. People steeped in satanism and the occult. As Blur confirmed for me, these people do have their own language, it's going to sound very weird unless we can help you in real time." He finished.

"Who is it that we need?" Hannah asked.

"We need to go to the Satanic Temple at City Hall Square and convince one of them to come with us. We need the humanist Satanists to help us out," Josh said.

The Devil is not as dark as he is painted. —Dante Alighieri

Chapter Five

We woke up early and made a quick run to the supermarket. We picked up a shopping cart full of canned food and then filled up a duffle bag that Jackson brought. The Satanic Temple on City Hall Square was having a canned food drive for the homeless and we wanted to make a nice first impression. We went back to my house to prep for the day.

"Ok, does everyone know what the plan is?" I asked.

"We need to locate one of them there who is willing to come with us on this insane trip. Any idea how we can go about doing that?" Rosette asked.

"I have an idea. I'm going to give them an occult quote and see if they know where it's from," Josh said.

"All we really need is to get it started up with someone and we'll be able to charm the hell out of them," Larisa said.

"Any reason you're wearing all black Graham?" Jackson asked. "You're not a priest and you might offend them by playing to a stereotype."

"I look great. What do you think Hannah?" I asked.

"Well, you still belong to the flat ass society," she said.

Rosette laughed.

"Shut up," I said through my laughter. "I thought the flat earth society was really nice," I said.

"They were, but this was a useful time to use them for a joke," Hannah said.

"All right everyone, let's get this show on the road," Larisa said.

We all packed into Jean's van. We made our way to City Hall Square. When we got there, we had to park a few blocks away because Boston traffic is awful.

"All right Jackson, grab the duffle bag and let's roll," I said.

He grabbed it and threw it over his back. Honestly, it looked like a backpack on him. I can't emphasize enough just how big this guy is.

We made our way to the address, 1 City Hall Square, and when we got there, people were already starting to load boxes of cans into their own van.

"How's it going?" one of them said to us. "Something I can help you with?"

"Hi, my name is Graham, and these are my friends. We wanted to drop off some canned goods for your drive." I said as I motioned to Jackson to hand the duffle bag to him. The guy tried to pick it up but couldn't, it was too heavy. He unzipped it and his eyes got wide.

"There's got to be hundreds of dollars' worth of food in here," he said.

"One hundred seventy dollars' worth to be exact," Josh said.

"Hey Eli, come over here and look at what these guys brought," The man said.

"Be right over Ant," Eli said.

Eli walked over and looked at the open duffel bag. His eyes got wide, and he looked up to us.

"Holy crap dude, you're Graham Newsdon," he said as he reached his hand out for mine.

"Who?" Ant said.

"Graham. You know, Into the Rabbit Hole series. The movies. Dude, I've never seen you around these parts, are you doing research for another book or something," he said as he smiled at me.

"Something like that. Actually, we were wondering if you would be able to take us inside so we can question a few of your members," I said.

"No problem. You know that since your books came out, there has been a huge bump in astrology and New World Order books. We've even seen bumps in our numbers in the church here. Not everyone understands Satanism, and most of them have different views on it, but we mostly adhere to the Eleven Satanic Rules of the Earth. Like, do not give opinions or advice unless you are asked. Do not tell your troubles to others unless you are sure they want to hear them. When in another's home, show them respect or else do not go there. Do not make sexual advances unless you are given the mating signal. Do not harm young children. Do not kill non-human animals unless you are attacked, or it's for your food. Stuff like that. Good, wholesome, honest, humanist things," Eli said.

Josh's eyebrows raised.

"Who was the depiction of Jesus based on?" He asked him.

Eli scratched his head. "I know most people think that it was Cesare Borgia, but I've heard that it was based on Apollonius of Tyana, so I'm not really sure," Eli said.

Josh smiled.

"Why is today special?" Josh asked.

"It's not really special for us per se, but it's May 8th, the White Lotus Day. The day of Madame Blavatsky's death," he said.

Josh smiled again.

"Is that why you guys are having a food drive today? To honor her?" Josh asked.

"We've had this planned for months, you'll have to ask the head inside," he said.

"Can we go meet them?" I asked.

Eli smiled and nodded.

"Graham Fucking Newsdon. It's awesome to meet you bro. Wait let me guess. You're Hannah, and you're Rosette. You're Jackson, you must be Larisa and you're Jean. Am I right?" He asked.

We smiled.

"All right guys, follow me," he said.

We walked past people putting cans into boxes while a Church protest was going on across the street. It seems that they had recently gotten the 10 commandments removed from city hall and were able to put a giant Baphomet statue up in the front of their building. Many of them smiled as they packed boxes full of cans.

We walked into the building and immediately bumped into a small group of 5 people. There was another group of 3 in the back of the room having coffee.

"All right guys, I'll handle these 5, you go to those 3 and ask them the same questions that I asked Eli before," he said.

We walked over to the group of three and kicked it with them for a few minutes. I asked them the questions, and none of them seemed to know. We said our good-byes to them and walked back to the middle of the room to meet up with Josh.

"None of them knew anything," I said.

"Mine neither," Josh said.

"What about Eli?" I asked.

Josh raised his eyebrows as if he hadn't thought of that before.

We walked around the room until we found him talking to one other person that we hadn't met. There were only ten people in this building.

"Hi Eli, how are you?" Josh began.

The man he was talking to turned to him.

"What is the meaning of this Astaroth?" He asked.

"It's fine Magog, don't worry about it. I'll handle it," he said

We looked confused as he led us a few feet away from I guess Magog.

"Hi guys. In here we use our Satanic name to address one another. There's like 4 Phils and 3 Mikes, it just gets confusing otherwise. Also, Magog is one of the more stringent believers in the law as opposed to the esoteric notion of it all. I'm Astaroth. Who forms the trinity with Beelzebub and Lucifer. You can call me Eli though. So, what can I help you guys with?" He asked.

I took a deep breath. "What do you know exactly about the Big Heaven Room?" I asked.

Eli's eyes got wide, and he got excited.

"You're going to break into there? I hadn't heard of anyone doing that since Blur did that a while back. What are you looking for?" He asked.

"It's not a what, it's a who. We're looking for the Pindar," Josh said.

Eli nodded his head, then cocked his head to the side as if to ask us to go outside with him. Once we got outside, he lit up a clove. Oh, thank God, I've been waiting for a cigarette for a while. I pulled out my half-crushed pack and lit one up.

"So, do you need something from me or what?" He asked.

"The thing is, these elites, these people who are Satanic by actual belief in a physical Satan, they speak in occult. It's not going to be enough for me to be there and I haven't brushed up on my Satanism in quite a while," Josh said.

"Wait, so you're asking me if I'd come with you to help you break in?" Eli asked.

"Baphomet is a knowledge rising in opposition to idolatry, protesting through the very monstrosity of the idol. The Israelites were forbidden to give divine concepts the figure of a man or of any animal; thus, on the ark of the covenant and in the sanctuary, they dared sculpt only cherubs, that is, sphinxes with the bodies of bulls and the heads of men, eagles or lions. These mixed figures reproduced neither the complete form of any man, nor that of any animal. These hybrid creations of impossible animals gave to understand that the image was not an idol or reproduction of a living thing, but rather a character or representation of something having its existence in thought. Baphomet is not worshipped." Josh said before he stalled out and opened his eyes wide and looked at Eli.

"It is God who is worshipped, this faceless God behind this formless form, this image which resembles no created being. Baphomet is not a God. He is the sign of initiation," Eli said.

"See, you've answered all the questions so far and you know an incredibly obscure Eliphas Levi quote. Out of everyone we've talked to here, you're perfect," Josh said.

"We'll pay you, and all your expenses will be paid for," Jean said.

Eli looked at them for a while and then broke out into a big smile.

"What's the worst that can happen. They bury me alive or put me in an acid bath? Sure, why not," Eli said.

"There's only one caveat to this," Jackson said.

"What's that?" He replied.

"You can't tell your Church where you're going. The only people that can know what's happening are in this circle right now," Jackson said.

Eli looked at him then looked down, took one final drag of his clove, clipped down to the filter and dropped it on the floor. He squished it out with his foot then looked up and blew smoke into the air.

"When do we leave?" He asked.

"We have two days to prepare everything. We can take you to your house where you can gather some supplies and clothes, and then bring you to my house where we're going to plan this thing," I said.

"All right, let me just ditch them inside, I'll be back in a few." He said as he went off inside.

"Go get the van Jean. We're going to have to squeeze this guy in somehow," Hannah said.

"Alright, just please make sure my woman doesn't take her clothes off while I'm gone," he said.

Larisa punched him in the arm. Rosette laughed.

"Is this what I'm really viewed as?" Larisa asked.

"Not really, but you do tend to get naked often when we're doing important things," Rosette said.

We waited for about 10 minutes. We were starting to think that Eli was not going to be coming back until he emerged behind us with a duffel bag.

"I already had a trip planned with them for a few days out of town, so I was already packed. I told them that my grandmother died overseas, and I was going to be out for a little while. Please bring me back in one piece," Eli said.

"No problem buddy," I said.

Just then Jean pulled around the bend with his van and we all got in. This clown car only seats 8, so we were perfect for now. Josh and Eli started talking back and forth about the truth in Satanism and Luciferianism. I tried to ignore them for the time being. I knew this would continue at the house. A few minutes into the car ride, Josh told me that we were going to have to have a crunch time lesson in Satanism and Luciferianism. Both he and Eli made it very clear that they were not the same thing. We would be prepping for the next day and then the following day we would be boarding Jean's plane to San Francisco. We didn't know what the Pindar was going to bring, but the one thing we didn't expect was the blind girl.

Paganism is wholesome because it faces the facts of life—Aleister Crowley

Chapter Six

We arrived at our house after about an hour in massive traffic. I opened the door, careful to disable the trip wire that was still there and let everyone upstairs. Once we got up there, Eli and I lit up a cigarette.

"So according to Blur, in the 1960's a company found a way to make a safer cigarette. It would heat the tobacco instead of lighting it on fire but was shelved by the cigarette companies who stood to lose money," Rosette said.

"You listen to Blur?" Eli asked.

I laughed.

"Blur is what conspiracy theorists call controlled oppo or controlled opposition. See everything is fine in conspiracy theories, until you amass too much of a following. Then their mentality goes from a truth teller to 'why the hell haven't you been murdered by the elite yet.' They accuse you of being controlled opposition. For instance, Graham you are considered controlled oppo because you're still alive. The anti-religion stories you put together on paper must serve some greater purpose to them. Basically, you and Blur are allowed to continue, but deep in the community they believe that you are a deceiver. When the elites find religion, the ones who call the shots tend to back off. It's all about optics. It gives the aura that these false Satanists will let their grasp go on them to keep the fiction of religion good and bad alive. They desperately need that dichotomy to exist, because without it, there couldn't be mass control. Blur is a Christian, which is why he's allowed to live. But if you had his massive platform, you would have been suicided by now," Eli said.

"Well, Graham makes us watch him. Anyway, Jax and I have to go home to pack. We'll see you in a couple of hours," Rosette said as she and Jackson made their way downstairs and outside.

"Yeah. Jean and I have to go back to our apartment too and pack. We'll be back in an hour or so," Larisa said as they left.

It was down to me, Eli and Josh.

"So what do you guys want to do in the meantime?" I asked.

"I'm going to go over some things that you need to know," Josh said.

"Did you know that the Church held what was called a 'Pink Mass' in July 2013. It was held over the grave of Fred Phelps, the head of the Westboro Baptist Church's mother. It had men kissing over the grave while a spell was put to change the deceased's sexual orientation," Eli said.

I snubbed out my cigarette in the cup of water left by our previous guest and laughed. "You won't believe the kind of trouble I've had with these people in the past," I said.

"I've seen it on the news, I think TMZ right?" Eli asked.

I nodded as I lit up another cigarette.

"So, are you going to talk or what?" I said turning to Eli.

"First you have to understand that in all pictures of Satan and Baphomet where they are holding two fingers together. I like your interpretation that it means they are a combination of two signs, but it goes back further than that. The ancient Kemetic sign for peace is a pointer and a middle finger together. Like they are posed. The European sign of war victory is the separation of those fingers to make the peace sign that people are familiar with this day and age," Eli said.

"Well, that's interesting for sure," I said.

"All mysteries of magic, all symbols of the gnosis, all figures of occultism, all kabbalistic keys of prophecy, are resumed in the sign of the Pentagram which Paracelsus proclaimed to be the greatest and most potent of all. It is indeed the sign of the absolute and universal synthesis.

That was written by Eliphas Levi, who was the first person to invert the pentagram. The inverted Pentagram is interesting. He was the first person to say that one point down and two points up was evil and one point up and two points down was good," he said.

"Many Satanists view the inverted cross as a symbol of theirs, but the truth is that it is not evil. It's considered St. Peter's cross. He asked to be crucified upside down because he didn't feel he deserved to die in the same manner that Jesus did," Josh said. "The inversion of an object can be traced back to that. It's actually a more humbling and higher regard," Josh said.

"Like those Knights Templar that had the Rosicrucian cross upside down on them, they just didn't know any better?" I asked.

"Exactly. Also, Eliphas was the first person to create Baphomet. He did it in dogmas and rituals of high magic in 1854," Josh said.

"You know your stuff Mason," Eli said.

"How can you tell?" Josh asked.

"The ring you refuse to take off for some reason," Eli said.

Josh looked down and took the ring off and put it on the desk.

"We're not on very good terms right now, Josh said.

"Levi was also famous for saying that in like manner, almost all popular superstitions are vulgar interpretations of some grand maxim or marvelous secret of occult wisdom," Josh said.

"There is nothing more to controlling demons than to do good and fear nothing. A little different than what the religious say isn't it?" Eli asked. "Basically Graham, Satanism is simply a literary declaration of defiance against arbitrary authority and the punishment of obedience. It punishes those ideas and people who wish to cage others from being their authentic selves. The idea of the Devil is an extremely old idea. There's a story of the Smith and the Devil which is a blacksmith who makes a deal with the devil in exchange for unmatched smithing powers. Very similar to Faust who sold his soul to the devil for 26 years of bliss. Anyway, the Smith and the Devil story can trace its way back to the proto-indo-european people. It's a 6000-year-old story. The interesting thing is that Satan has always been depicted in our mind as red with the devil horns and tail. The oldest surviving image of Satan is actually blue. It's a 6th century piece. It's in the Basilica of Sant'Apollinare Nuovo in Ravenna, Italy. Jesus appears in royal purple robes to save the saved from the damned. You'll find this interesting Graham. The damned were shown as goats standing with Blue Satan and the saved were the sheep. Astrotheologically how would you interpret that, bud?"

"I'd say that the goat is Capricorn, and the dead of winter which makes it evil, and the sheep represent Aries which is the start of the Zodiac, the beginning of spring and the return of the Sun," I said.

"I had a feeling you would say something like that," Eli said.

"Baphomet did become popularized as well as his image because of Levi but weren't the Knights Templars accused of worshipping him and were all killed October 13, 1307, which is where we get the Friday the 13th superstition from. Baphomet comes from the word Abufihamat which means father of wisdom and was applied to King Solomon," Josh said.

"Yes, but what you don't know is that Baphomet represents both male and female as one. Have you ever noticed what a nice pair of tits he has on him?" Eli asked.

I laughed.

"So Lucifer literally means the light bringer. The light bearer, the bringer of dawn, the shining one or morning star and has always been applied as you know Graham to the planet Venus. Thus, the Christians who claim that Lucifer is the Devil actually have no Biblical basis or authority for such a belief. Yet who can deny that even Jesus is portrayed as boldly proclaiming his identity with Venus, the Light Bringer, in Revelation 22:16 where he says 'I Jesus am the bright and morning star.' If the translators had chosen to translate this verse using Latin just as they did with Isaiah 14:12, it would read 'I Jesus, am Lucifer.' That was Madame Blavatsky who created Theosophy. Today is the day of her death. Those in the know, know that Lucifer is not the Devil and is not evil. The Vatican even has a telescope named Lucifer," Eli said.

"Also, Satan in Hebrew means 'adversary' not the Devil, evil etc. This is all the truth that is hidden unless you search for it. The religious Christians have perverted it to their own benefit. Just as they've said that astrology is witchcraft. That H.P. Lovecraft's Necronomicon is pure evil. Anything they don't like is Satanism. It's a quick fix. Satan or Lucifer is not regarded as the embodiment of evil. To worship a being of true evil is regarded as the act of a psychopath for Luciferians and Satanists. Luciferians and Satanists view Christians as victims of their own religion, too dependent on their religion to escape from it. Luciferians do not see their choices as acts of rebellion, but instead, believe themselves to be motivated by independent thought. Luciferians also tend to see Satanists as overly dependent on Christian understandings. As a Luciferian perspective goes, Satanists embrace values such as pleasure, success and sexuality because that's exactly what the Christian Church has taught against. All things that Aleister Crowley wrote about. They ended up calling him the wickedest man that ever lived. Luciferians view Satanists as being primarily focused on the physical nature of man, exploring, experimenting and enjoying that nature while rejecting any aspirations or effort to rise beyond it," Josh said.

"Well, that's where Satanists and I disagree. I'd consider myself more of a Luciferianist, but I'm trying to work my understanding in the Church so they can open their eyes a bit," Eli said.

"Satan is Saturn. Binah on the tree of life. These are all the same: manifestation, time, space, materiality, limitation. Hence Satanism to the actual magicians is the 'worship' of all these aspects of reality above all else. This would not be the LaVey Satanism which is basically inverted Catholicism. This is the 'Satanists' that Blur Slanders talks about. Greed, war, adrenochrome etc. Lucifer is the same as Prometheus, both of whom go against nature/the gods to achieve new technologies for the advancement of man, despite the consequences," Josh said.

"Graham, the reason why certain religions, take your pick, teach that yoga and meditation are 'demonic and satanic' is because what happened hundreds of years ago. When Britain invaded India, they had trouble controlling the population, who were very in tune with their bodies. Due to a dedicated ancient Yoga and Meditation, Kundalini practices, what have you, many Indians developed 'Siddhis' which are special abilities unexplained by modern science such as telekinesis, psychic and shamanic power. Much like what you're starting to see with all these Starseed and Indigo children being born in this new age. This is why the control system had the church teach that yoga and meditation were evil, to try and stop others from developing these innate human abilities, which threaten their control. Satanists and Luciferianists believe that the 'self' is the most important thing in the World, in stark contrast with religions and their belief in serving God comes first," Eli said.

He had mentioned Starseed and Indigo children. There was that word again, Starseed. I couldn't help but think that it had something to do with what we were looking for.

"I've heard that Satanism is more about pleasure," I said.

"That depends how you look at it. Theistic Satanism is not just about carnal pleasure of the Aleister Crowley nature. It's more about a balance between the carnal and spiritual, the 'dark' energy and the 'light' energy, because one cannot exist without the other. That's why they say that Satan is the man of light but is also the prince of darkness. Luciferianism focuses only on the light side, whereas the Church of Satan focuses on the dark one. Luciferianism is also more or less a worship of a light-bringing entity. It does not really believe that Lucifer is evil, because to worship something truly evil would be appalling to either of them," Eli said.

"Wait, going back to Eliphas Levi and the Pentagram, in Astrotheology, God I feel like I've said this a million times, the Pentagram is the earth and Venus's 5 points where they are the closest together in their revolution around the Sun," I said.

"Yes, that's true, but there's more than one way to skin a cat Graham," Josh said.

"I've heard you say that in your lectures before, Josh is right," Eli said.

"So why go against God?" I asked.

"Graham, when you consider that God could have commanded anything he wanted. The Ten Commandments have got to rank as one of the great missed moral opportunities of all time. How different would history have been had he clearly and unmistakably forbidden war, tyranny, taking over other people's countries, slavery, exploitation of workers, cruelty to children, wife-beating, stoning, treating women or anyone as chattel or inferior beings as Katha Politt puts it. If you take the Bible literally, God has killed himself over a million people, or commanded people to do so. Satan has committed maybe 10? There's no comparison. Satanism is simply a literary declaration of defiance against arbitrary authority and the punishment of obedience. It punishes in return those ideas and people who wish to cage others from being their authentic selves. It's the Hegelian dialectic. You create a problem, sin, and say that no man or woman can escape from it. We're all sinners and we're all going to fall short of perfection. We are punished for that. Then the idea that all you have to do is believe in the Resurrection and give your heart to Jesus, and you're saved for all eternity. It's simple, everyone can do it. They believe that people cannot find salvation though learning, reading, studying. The more ignorant you are, the better off you are. Satanism and Luciferianism are the opposite of that. From the beginning, Satan intervened to give people the chance to collect knowledge and illuminate themselves. What is more absurd and more impious than to attribute the name of Lucifer to the devil, that is, to personified evil. I can't stress enough that the idea of Lucifer and the Devil are not the same. Religious people would know that if they cracked a book. The intellectual Lucifer is the spirit of intelligence and love. It is the paraclete. It is the Holy Spirit, while the physical Lucifer is the great agent of universal magnetism, which in contrast with the male electric, is of the feminine nature. Walter Russell talks about this constantly in his writings, that everything is just based electric or magnetic. The other thing that the Satanic Temple rejects, Graham, is attempts at reproductive enslavement by religious zealots. Theocrats are aggressively pushing laws that prohibit abortion and deprive American citizens of basic bodily autonomy. These violate the Temple's Third Tenet which states 'One's body is inviolable, subject to one's own will alone. Also, on a completely different note, it's important to know that Satan wasn't always portrayed as an evil, beastly monster. In the Romantic era of the late 18th and early 19th centuries, revolutionary writers and artists reimagined the character of Satan in the epic poem 'Paradise Lost' as a hero, daring to rebel against God's unjust tyranny. This gave way to writers such as Anatole France whose work was banned by the Church and his books burned," Josh said.

"That must be my favorite book I own," Eli said.

"What book?" I asked.

"It's called the Revolt of the Angels. It's a Satanic masterpiece. Probably the most important novel written against God and religion. The revolt of the angels is treasured by LaVey and the church of Satan. The story is about a group of angels who rebel and plot together to retake heaven. Lucifer says, "Comrades, we must be happy and rejoice, for behold, we are delivered from celestial servitude.' We still must needs congratulate ourselves on having known pain, for pain has revealed to us new feelings, more precious and sweeter than those experienced in eternal bliss, and inspired us with love and pity unknown in Heaven," You see, at the time, Heaven was considered eternal endless bliss. A most high of vibrational energy. You experience higher vibrations through orgasm. Satan finally figures out that the real battle is not external, but internal to every man, demon and seraph. We must overcome our own jealousy, fear, superstition and ignorance as well as to cultivate wisdom, compassion, curiosity and the love of arts and beauty instead. See Graham, it's all about putting the self over everything. Religious people will say no matter what you learn and figure out in your journeys and astrology writings, none of it will ever be good enough because it doesn't glorify God. This is about glorifying the self," Eli said. "The problem is that most of the elite of elites believe in a perversion of Satanism. Where he is a real entity, and they make sacrifices to. This is not the case at all. I've never met a single Satanist or Luciferian who didn't understand this. Most of these people are psychopaths. Good chance these people were bathed in serotonin during fetal development and have become resistant to it," Eli said.

Just then we heard some noise coming from downstairs.

“What did we miss bitches?” Rosette asked as she smiled, Jackson holding two duffle bags above his head.

“Are you moving in or what?” I asked.

“No silly, I just picked up some things we need to go over,” Rosette said as Jean and Larisa followed shortly behind.

“What have you guys been talking about?” Larisa asked.

“Just a lot of Satanism and Luciferianism stuff. It’s really interesting. Been completely perverted by the Church and the religious for centuries. Jackson, what do you think happens when we die?” I asked.

“There’s a theory known as quantum immortality in which the mind will always transport itself to alternate realities where it survives otherwise fatal events. Conservation of energy, matter cannot be created or destroyed. I have no idea what happens when we die, but it’s hard to dismiss all these NDE’s,” Jackson said.

“You’re talking about Near Death Experiences?” Eli asked.

Jackson nodded.

“All right guys, let’s go over what I have here. OK, so first, I have an RFID Card Copier in case you’re able to slip someone’s card away for a second, I can clone it and it'll allow you into the buildings. Secondly, and this is important, whoever finds the Pindar, I have this thing," Rosette said as she pulled out what looked like a mosquito.

"What the hell is that Rosette?" I asked.

"It's an insect spy drone. It's remotely controlled and is equipped with a camera and a microphone. It can implant an RFID tracking chip into her, so we won't have to constantly be chasing around for her," she said.

"That's great stuff Rose. Are you able to get into the compound with your computer?" I asked.

"I looked into it, it's pretty locked down. I would have to physically be at the computer to do anything, but I did bring an Air Selfie," she said.

"I suppose you're going to tell us what that is?" I asked.

"It's a 2oz flying camera that can fit in your pocket. I'm going to scan the entire compound with it and transmit the information back. Here, you're all going to want to wear these as well." She said as she handed out pairs of glasses.

"What are these?" Jean asked.

"These are prototypes from the government. Remember Google Glass? These are thirty times faster. We can network link up on them like a group chat and see what everybody is seeing. Like a multiplayer video game. The audio comes from the earpieces we have," she said.

"Do you have any other tricks up your sleeve?" Rosette asked.

"I might have one or two others, but I don't know if I'll need them or be able to use them," she said. "Make sure you go to the bathroom before you enter the compound. I saw a small pond nearby, and unless you're going to swim with the fish, I don't think you should hold it,"

I laughed.

"What's so funny?" Jean asked.

"I was just thinking about my high school senior prank with NP. We skipped every class except for gym and went to the pet store and bought a bunch of tiny fish, rocks, decorations for a fish tank. Clever Interlock only was 2 floors high and had two bathrooms. We went into the men's bathroom and shut the door, then we filled all the toilets with gravel and fish. On both floors. We clogged the sinks and did the same there. You had to see the look on people's faces when they would burst in to have to take a dump and see the fish," I said hysterically laughing.

"That's terrible, Graham. Those poor fish," Hannah said.

"It was amazing. We were against the wall outside the first-floor bathroom talking, and we'd hear people yelp and scream when they saw it. They had to call the maintenance man." I stopped as I couldn't finish my sentence.

"Alright, does anybody have an idea on how to create a diversion?" Larisa asked.

"I do," I said as I went back into my room and brought back a jar of pills.

"What is that exactly?" Jackson asked.

"It's nitric oxide," I said.

"You trying to get a pump from lifting?" Jackson asked.

"Not exactly. This stuff increases clitoral blood flow and can make men's erections super hard. It comes on out of nowhere. If they are going to drink adrenochrome, I'm going to pour these into the pot. It'll be a fuck frensy in no time," I said.

"That's a strangely good idea," Rosette said.

"Only thing is, when people start shacking up with each other, we need to locate the Pindar. We still don't know how that is going to happen," I said.

"We'll figure it out bud," Jackson said.

"Also, I do have a Zip Bomb," Larisa said.

"What is that?" Rosette asked.

"So glad you asked that sweetie," she said as she winked at her.

Rosette giggled.

"This takes a 46 MB file to 4.5 petabytes. It'll completely fry the server if I can find it. Might put them out of commission while they're all out having sex, snorting coke, drinking blood, whatever," Larisa said.

"You sure you can do this?" Jackson asked.

"If a hacker broke into NASA using a Raspberry Pi, I'm sure I can handle this honey," Larisa said.

"Alright guys, so we're all good to go. I have two black Escalades waiting for us at SFO. We better go. Wheels up in an hour," Jean said.

We all got our bags and piled into Jean's van. The adrenaline was rushing, but something truly bothered me. We had no idea what we were looking for. Something terrible was going to happen and we were in the dark. It amazes me how many people in the world just go about their daily lives not knowing the insane things that go on behind the scenes. Truth is, finding the Pindar was going to be an impossible mission I thought as I shaved my head in the back seat of the car into a plastic bag. I was going to have to blend in. Truth is we all would have ended up dead had it not been for that blind girl.

If one were to take the bible seriously, one would go mad. But to take the Bible seriously, one must be already mad. —Aleister Crowley.

Chapter Seven

We got out at SFO and had two Escalades waiting for us. We split up and got in. I punched the directions for the location of the Big Heaven Room, and we made our way. Lucky for us there was a hotel a mile away from it. We went in and made reservations under Danger Showman, which is an anagram for me. We set up in two adjoining rooms, then met back in my room.

"It's do or die time guys. Are we all ready?" I asked.

"I'm so ready. Wait, who's sneaking in and who's staying back?" Larisa asked.

"Me and Jackson are definitely staying back. He'd stick out like a sore thumb. Plus, it could be a racist environment too. Never know with these old ass people," Rosette said.

"I'm staying back too. I'll run comms from the trucks," Jean said.

"We'll stay back too. If you locate the Pindar, you'll need help translating what she says," Josh said about him and Eli.

"Great, so it's me and Larisa I guess," I said.

"Try not to have too much fun this time Larisa," Jean said.

She turned and smiled at him. "I know what we have to get done sweetie," she said.

"All right guys, so we're going to pile into the cars and I'm going to get as close to the woods as I can. Everyone put on your earpiece and DigiOptix glasses," Jean said.

It took us a few minutes to set up, but eventually we were good. These glasses don't look conspicuous at all and the comms in our ears weren't showing. They have these mini ear buds now. They are really remarkable.

Jean and Jackson drove us to the location and backed up into the woods across the street from where we needed to go. Larisa and I got out.

"Alright guys, testing. Can everybody hear me?" I asked.

"Loud and clear. Larisa you good?" Jean asked.

"Rock and roll baby," she said.

"Rosette?" I asked.

"I'm here Graham," she said.

"Josh and Eli, are you guys there?" Larisa asked.

"We're here," they said.

"How do I look guys?" I asked.

"Since you shaved your head and shaped up your beard, you literally look nothing like you. You'll be fine," Jackson said.

"Alright Larisa, let's go," I said.

Larisa had a small backpack with all our supplies. She bounced through the trees snapping away at her bubble gum. I kept thinking that she's going to have a better chance at isolation with the Pindar than I am.

"Alright guys, where do we go?" I asked.

"Go around the pond in front of you and keep walking straight. You should get there in five minutes," Jean said as he saw through our glasses what we were seeing.

"So Riss, how you been?" I asked.

"Not bad. I've been doing some work with Anonymous on bringing down some pedophile groups on the deep web. Just trying to stay busy you know," she said.

Truth was I didn't know. I had no idea about the dark Web and that was the first time I ever heard of the Mariana web. I'd sooner leave this to professionals. We walked for another five minutes, and we came across a sight that we'd never forget.

There was a set of semicircle seating like an arena. There were people in robes surrounding a round table at the front all holding knives. They were 20 feet away from us all holding knives. The stage was lit in stark contrast with the darkness surrounding us. We sat down in a seat. People started to file in and sit around us. There was a robe like the ones they were wearing up front, I picked it up and folded it and used it as a seat cushion. Might come in handy later.

One of the men that I recognized from Congress was running around bugging out that he couldn't find his robe. Another man stood up and pointed to the building behind us, well it was more like a log cabin really. The man went in and when he came out, he had another robe. It was clear to me that I had just stolen his robe that he set down. Larisa opened her backpack and took out the small flying camera/drone. She guided it into the sky and started moving it around. It was so small nobody would be able to see it in the darkness.

"OK guys, I'm giving you a full site visual. Get back to me with what you see," she whispered into her comm.

"Copy that," Jackson said.

Just then a small child, about 2-3 years old was brought out and put on the round table. A chill went up my spine.

"You've got to be kidding me. Are you guys seeing this?" I asked.

"Keep calm Graham. You knew damn well this was a possibility," Josh said.

I suddenly had an urge for a cigarette. I took one out of my pocket and lit it up. The sky lit up in a gray line. I sat back a little and tried to settle my stomach. Larisa started fumbling around with her backpack. She was moving her hands around and it looked like she was looking for something.

"Need help?" I whispered to her.

"No Graham, it's fine, I'm just running a wide range bug scanner. So far nothing. These people, whoever they are, are good at keeping recording devices out of here." She said as she pulled out a Zippo lighter and a grape swisher sweet from her bag.

"What the hell are you doing? You don't smoke," I said.

"I do tonight," she said as she pointed to the Zippo, then to me and made a taking a picture motion with her hand. She has a hidden camera in a cigarette lighter. She never ceases to amaze me.

"You do know Graham," she started as she lit up her cigar, "that the cigarette lighter came out three years before the match," she said as she cocked her mouth to the side and blew the smoke out.

"I actually did know that. Why are you smoking?" I asked again.

"Rosette said psychologically it's sexual signaling. I'm hoping to befriend a guy here who can lead me to the Pindar," she said.

Larisa with the sexual mojo again. This can't be good.

"Just don't have the sex!" Jean screamed into the comms. We turned and winced as he was quite loud with that one.

"Come on now Jean," she said.

Just then the bulk of people came sitting down. Some with robes, some without. I made a snap call judgment and quickly put on the robe. I grabbed the bottle of nitric oxide from the bag and dumped the pills into my pocket. I pulled up the hoodie on it and sat back down. California in the Spring with a hoodie on around a giant fire. This is hell on Earth.

"Anybody with any news on the camera?" Larisa asked.

"We have camp names. There's a list that you can find in front of the building behind you. Looks like a sign on sheet. Has the names of the people and where they stay after the ceremony. The camps are 'Prism Veneers, Townless, Many A Lad, Libs Lie Hill, Acme Stir, Ciao Stir.' She's going to be in one of those. Just look at the names when you get up to go to the bathroom or something," Jean said.

"Doesn't look like we're getting a bathroom break anytime soon," I said as I looked around. There was a young girl, likely the youngest person here aside from the baby who was sitting on a chair, stimming. She looked like she had no idea where she was. After observing her for a short time, I realized that she was blind. My attention was soon turned around to the stage, where a giant 20-foot bumble bee statue was erected. Just then a man came in a black robe. Everybody else was wearing red robes and red shoes. Wait, what the hell was going on?

"Josh, Eli, what's the deal with the red shoes?" I asked.

"The red shoes are an evil perversion of Satan/Satanic symbol of child sacrifice," Eli said.

"I didn't want to know that." Larisa said as she finished up in her bag. "All done. Looks like these private rooms are bugged, but not out here," she said.

"HEY, you two are in my spot!" A voice growled behind me.

I stood up and turned around and saw an extremely famous musician. My jaw dropped.

"Yes, I know kid, just get out of my way, ok?" He asked.

I motioned to Larisa to stand up. We walked around the curve and sat down at the left edge of it, far away from this guy. Just then, the man in the black robe started to speak.

"We honor you great bee, for without you, we have nothing on Earth." He began. Just then my head flashed back to DeBerg as the beekeeper. Was he here at one point of his life?

"Mundus vult decipi, ergo decipiatur. Mundus vult decipi, ergo decipiatur," the man said.

Just then the entire audience repeated the same thing.

"Guys, I'm going to need a translation on that," I said softly into my comm.

"Working on it hold on. Ok, it means 'The World wants to be deceived, so let it be deceived'," Rosette said.

"No crap," I said as I adjusted my glasses.

"Please brother, bring me the Lapsit," the man in the black said.

One of the men next to him slowly started walking towards us and stopped at a crate that was besides us that we hadn't even noticed. He opened it and I keeled over to get a good look at it. The man looked at me and smiled and brought it towards the man in black.

"Graham, that's the Lapsit Exillis. It's the stone that broke off Lucifer's crown during his plunge to Earth," Eli said.

"I thought they weren't real," Rosette said.

"These people believe that they are real darling. They're very dangerous," Josh said.

The man lifted it up to the air and the crowd bowed their heads in unison for a few moments and prayed. I looked around and I saw the child was starting to get fidgety. Just then the man in black put down the stone and took a dagger out of his pocket.

"We present to you an offering. We take what's ours. Do what thou wilt," he said.

"Do what thou wilt," everyone repeated in unison.

Just then I witnessed a sight I never thought I would see. The child was laid out on the circle, but the table had holes in it. One by one, the 9 people up there surrounded the child and in one swoop, speared their daggers through the holes and through the child. Blood splattered everywhere, but more noticeable was that it was draining directly under him into a bucket that looked to be half full already. Once the child stopped crying and moving, the man in black ushered in a man sitting in the front row to take the child, which he did. The man and the child disappeared into one of the cottages behind us. Then the man in black took the bucket and grabbed a sleeve of plastic shot glasses. He handed the bucket over to the farthest person on the left, just a few seats down from us. The bucket had a lot of blood in it, clearly more than that child just produced. This was just for optics and effects.

"It's like Lenin said, the best way to control the opposition is to lead it ourselves. Enjoy the night brothers and sisters," the man said as he took his hoodie off. My jaw dropped for the second time in half an hour. It was Labac Hamashiach Morgenstern, the head of the Consortium.

A few years back there was a deadly virus that originated in China. It spread through the world and people were dying off. This was before the Jellyfish vaccine situation. Borders were closing and the world was in rough shape. It brought people back together, helping each other every way we could. Eventually when the virus started to die down, the EU expanded as per people begging to embrace one another. It was made out of love, but eventually the Consortium was founded. Countries in the East started joining them. The conspiracy theorists theorized that it was the start of a one world government, the New World Order.

Just then the bucket was passed to Larisa, she poured some into her shot glass and handed me the bucket. Everybody was now talking amongst themselves, and nobody was paying us much attention, so as quickly as I could, I dumped the pills into the bucket and shook the bucket from side to side. The pills evaporated nearly instantly. I took a shot glass full and passed the bucket to the next person. Larisa and I stood up and went back to the cottage we were originally at, my hoodie still up, and we were stopped by the blind girl.

"Not a big fan of the refreshments?" She asked with a deep almost manly voice.

"Wait, you can see us?" I asked.

"Of course, I can see you. You two aren't from around here, are you?" She asked.

I was shocked. I could have sworn she was blind. "Who are you?" I asked.

She looked over at me and laughed. "My name is Venga. I'm the protector of Baba," she said in a low voice.

"Who's Baba?" Larisa asked.

"She's the one I protect. You made her nervous before, she's never seen you," Venga said.

"I don't understand," I said.

"You're not supposed to. She is the daughter of the head of the Consortium. I started protecting her around the time her father and his friends started crawling into her bed at night. When she gets scared, she just calls for me," Venga said.

"Well, that's good I suppose," I said.

We looked up and saw a woman in a cocktail dress sauntering up to us a little drunk it seemed. She scratched her left ankle where she had a unique tattoo I'd never seen before.

"Hey, do either of you have anymore juice?" She asked me.

“Here, take mine,” Larisa said.

Her eyes grew wide as she took Larisa’s and downed it, then looked me up and down and took mine and downed it as well. After what seemed like a few minutes, she began to calm down.

“Excuse me dear, would you be a doll and help me to my room?” She asked Larisa rather loudly.

Not wanting to stand out or make a scene, Larisa took her hand and began to lead her.

“Who are you exactly?” Larisa asked.

“Nobody cares about me anymore. Nobody cares about Amrita St. Clair anymore,” she said.

I took my hood off and looked at Larisa. I nodded in approval for her to walk this lady over to whatever room she’s in.

“What room are you staying in?” Larisa asked.

“I’m in Ciao Stir. Do be a doll and help me out,” Amrita said.

Larisa took off and it was just me. Venga started snickering behind me.

“You know how this is going to end with her? The same way it always ends with her. Your friend is going to disappear unless she can prove she belongs here,” Venga said.

A chill ran up my spine.

"What do you mean unless she belongs here?" I asked.

I turned around to look at her and once again it seemed like she couldn't see anything. So odd.

"What did you mean by what you just said to me?" I asked.

"Who are you? What's happening?" She said but now in a soft girl's voice.

"We were just talking for the last 10 minutes. You don't remember?" I asked.

"I don't I'm sorry. I'm not supposed to talk to strangers. Daddy says it could get me in trouble one day." She said as she looked around trying to find my voice then started sucking on her thumb.

I have no clue what's going on here.

"Ask her for her name Newsdon," Rosette said.

"What's your name sweetie?" I asked.

"My name is Baba. My daddy takes me here every year and has a big party," she said.

I took a step back. "Your dad is the head of the Consortium?" I asked.

She nodded her head.

"Newsdon, this might be our only shot. You have to convince her to come with you so that I can assess her. She might have some information in her that might lead us to the Pindar," Rosette said.

"I don't know what's going on Rose," I said.

"Who are you talking to? I don't hear anybody else," Baba said.

"Never mind. Listen, I want to help you. Would you be willing to come with me and meet some of my friends?" I asked.

She got all fidgety. "Last time I met some friends, they touched me in my privates," Baba said.

My heart sank for her. "Well, my friends are not like that, and we can help you out. I promise," I said.

"No! I won't go. Daddy says to sit right here until he gets back. Sometimes his friends bring me some juice that tastes funny," Baba said.

"I have a very special friend that would love to meet you. It will not be that long. Can you please come with me?" I pleaded.

Suddenly her demeanor changed. Just like that, she was able to see again.

"She said no. Scram before I make somebody here make you wish you were never born," she said. Venga must be back.

"Venga, please, you have to listen to me. I'm here with some friends and something incredibly terrible is about to happen that's going to decimate the planet. There won't be anything left for us if we don't talk to Baba," I said.

Venga laughed. “Do you have any idea what kind of hell we’re already living in. If this is the end of civilization, then I’m fine with that,” she said.

“It would only be for a short time. We just need to get some information about the Pindar,” I said.

Venga stopped laughing. “The Pindar. I haven’t heard that word in a very long time. I don’t know how much help I can be, I’ve never met her, or if I did, had no clue who she was,” Venga said.

“All we want is a chance to talk to her,” I pleaded.

“I’m sorry, but you need to get out of here,” she said.

Frustrated and upset I started to collect myself to leave when I heard Rosette’s voice.

“Tell her your name,” she said.

“What? I asked into the comm.

“Your name,” she said.

Venga looked puzzled. “You’re not supposed to be here, are you?” She asked loudly.

“Please Venga, listen. I’m Graham. Graham Newsdon, I said. I was about to say more, but the look on her face said it all.

“You’ve got to be kidding me. THE Graham Newsdon. You broke into here? Your balls must be stone cold boy. What are you doing here?” She asked.

I was shocked she knew who I was, but I had to keep it going. Some people were noticing us talking for a bit of time.

"Something very bad is going to happen," I started repeating myself.

"Yeah, yeah, I get it. But what are YOU doing here?" Venga asked.

"I'm here to find out what's going to happen. I have it on good intelligence that this meeting here was called after Betelgeuse turned Supernova as it was a celestial sign the elites needed. Someone at this meeting knows what's going on, whether it's Baba's father or the Pindar, we just need to figure it out," I said.

Venga looked me over for a bit and then smiled and bit her lip. "I liked you better with hair and clean shaven. Where are your friends?" She asked.

"In two trucks by the entrance by the pond," I said.

Venga looked around left and right. "All right. I'll come, but if she starts to get uncomfortable or asks me to come out, we're done," she said.

"I understand," I said.

Just as I said that, the guests there started getting a bit rowdy. The women started fanning themselves and holding their breasts. The men couldn't stop hopping up and down. The nitric oxide was working. Male and Female Viagra hardcore. They started grabbing whoever they could and dragging them to these cabins. The orgy fest was about to commence. I just had to sneak Venga out.

I took my robe and put it on her, covering her head with the hood. She smiled at me. We had to sneak around the long way to get back to the car, but we eventually were able to sneak past the straggling people who just decided to have sex where they had been standing. I don't think anybody saw us in the confusion. Plus, I'm pretty sure I saw Labac go into one of the rooms with a group of people. After a few minutes, we were at the van. Rosette introduced herself to her, and they went in one car alone. The rest of us went into the other van. Then it hit me. Larisa.

To practice magic is to be a quack; to know magic is to be a sage—Eliphas Levi

Chapter Eight

"Guys, I have to go back," I said as I looked to my friends.

"You can't. We can't guide you back safely without running into people at this point. Larisa still has the mini drone," Jackson said.

"I don't care, I have to. It might take me a little while longer, but I have to," I said as I opened the car and stepped out.

"Graham, if you go, we can't save you if you get caught," Josh said.

I sat for a second and then thought.

"I'm taking the robe back from Venga, or Baba or whatever her name is. I'll be right back," I said as I got out of the car and walked to the car next to me and knocked on the door. After a long pause Rosette came out looking flustered.

"Graham what?" She asked. Uh oh, she never calls me Graham.

"I need the robe. I forgot Larisa, I have to go back," I said.

Rosette's eyes got wide and fumbled around the car. She tossed it out the door.

"Don't come in here, I'm about to start the therapy," she said as she shut the door.

Therapy? What therapy?

I didn't even say goodbye to them, I just took off running. When I got to the pond, I noticed there were some people around it talking and laughing. There was a couple 5 feet from them having sex on the ground. I looked closer. This was the musician and a male stripper on the floor. They were both covered in blood. I pulled my hood down and walked slowly past them hoping not to interact.

"Guys I'm going dark. I need to work on this girl. Ciao!" Rosette said.

"You got it," I said.

"Where are you headed brother?" One of them asked me.

Crap.

"I'm out of the magic juice. I'm heading back," I said, distorting my voice.

"Hell yeah, bring us back some when you come back." The man said as he walked up to the two of them on the floor and slapped one of them in the ass. "Get back to work you two," he said laughing.

I started picking up my pace a little faster. After another 15 minutes of carefully avoiding people, I ended up where Larisa was. I could see that because I could see myself walking to her through our glasses group chat. I sat down on the floor behind what I could only describe as a tree house.

"Riss I'm back," I said.

I could see her nodding up and down in the glasses.

"Alright guys, our earpieces are still in but we're going offline on the camera goggles. It's too busy," Jackson said as everybody disconnected except me, Larisa and Rosette. The screens got bigger and I was able to see more clearly. If I only knew what was about to happen.

"Why did you kill that little boy?" Larisa asked.

"Relax, God has seen your tears and heard your prayers. Fear not the child will not die," Amrita St. Clair said.

"That's a famous line from Aleister Crowley guys," Eli jumped in.

"You a fan of Mr. Crowley I see," Larisa said to her.

Amrita turned to her and smiled. "Child, I think you might be the first person who has ever known where that came from. What's your name again?" She asked Larisa.

"My name is not important. I'm here to seek out the Pindar," Larisa said.

Amrita's eyes got wide open and smiled. "Oh, you are? What makes you think I'll bring you to her," she said.

"For this," Larisa said as she took her glasses off and placed them on the desk aimed at them. She took her cigarette lighter out of her pocket and a swisher sweet as well. She lit up the cigar, then placed the Zippo on the table by Amrita.

Perfect, now we have a 360 view of the room and them. I just hope that one of them can record.

"What is that tattoo on your leg?" Larisa asked as she unzipped her sweatshirt and put it down on the bed and smiled at Amrita.

"This old thing, this is the old ways," Amrita said.

We got a good look at her tattoo this time, it seemed like something from Kabbalah, but I wasn't familiar with it.

"Graham, we need to talk," Rosette said.

"What's up?" I whispered back.

"I've been speaking to this girl for a little bit. From what I can tell, she's got MPD, trichotillomania and something called conversion disorder. This would take a lifetime to undo, but I'm going to keep trying," she said.

"In English please?" Josh said.

"Right, sorry. She's got multiple personality disorder. From what I can gather, it started when she was molested as a young kid. It also stunted her mental growth, which is why she talks like a kid. She also has a habit of pulling her hair out when she's Baba. Venga came in as one of her personalities to protect Baba. I haven't made much progress with Venga, but she's allowing me to speak to Baba. Conversion disorder is a tricky thing to explain, but basically this girl is not blind. But for some reason she only presents with blindness with her actual self. Venga can see perfectly well. I've been trying Erickson's waking hypnosis to work on her. It's basically hypnosis while you are still awake. You start by shaking their hand, in an awkward way, I can't get into it right now. Just know I'm working on this. How long until Larisa's back?" She asked.

"I don't know. She's playing a cat and mouse game with this lady. As long as she doesn't try and do anything horrible, we'll just deal with it," I said.

"Alright, keep me posted," Rosette said.

I watched Larisa and Amrita talking for a few. Every time something came up that she didn't know, Josh or Eli were right there to help her out. I could see through the glasses that Amrita was getting hot and bothered.

"Let me give you something child. Tell me what you make of this?" Amrita said as she took her sweatshirt off and threw it on the bed. She was wearing a white tank top and you could see that her nipples were rock hard under them.

"Be careful Riss," I said.

Larisa was given a piece of paper and held it up to her face so we could all see.

> **Aye! Listen to the numbers & the words: 4 6 3 8 A B K 2 4 A L G M O R 3 Y xZ 24 89 RPST OVAL. What meaneth this, o prophet? Thou knowst not; nor shalt thou know ever.**

I took a screenshot of this and kept it on my viewing screen.

"I'll get back to you soon Riss," I said.

"That's a line from Aleister Crowley's book," Eli said.

"Another Crowley puzzle. Do you think I could have a few minutes to look it over?" Larisa said as she winked at Amrita.

"Do what thou wilt darling," Amrita said. "I'm just going to have another drop of the serum," she said.

"Wait don't do that. I have something that's better for you." Larisa said as she walked over to Amrita and took her hand and sat her down on the bed. Out of her back pocket she pulled out an EpiPen. This must have been the oxidized one discussed a while back. How the hell did she get a hold of one? She lifted Amrita's skirt just a little bit to expose her inner thigh, then stabbed her with it and pushed the juice inside.

Within 20 seconds Amrita was flying high. She arched her back on the bed and ran her hands over her breasts and down her stomach. She looked over at Larisa and laughed and bit her lip.

"Oh no, she's going to try and sleep with her now," Jean said.

I laughed. I really don't understand how it's always Larisa.

"Come here child. Let me take you on an adventure," Amrita said.

"Graham hurry," Larisa whispered.

Larisa slowly made her way to Amrita and laid down on top of her. She smiled at her.

"Once I figure this puzzle out, you're going to help me find the Pindar, right?" She said as she teased Amrita's hair.

"What did you inject me with child. This is the most amazing feeling. It's like the serum but times a hundred," she said.

"It's an oxidized Epinephrine pen. It's the same high you get, only without having to kill anybody for it,"

Larisa said as she slid down Amrita to her crotch and then pushed herself up and went back to the desk.

"Can you get me more of this?" She asked.

"I've got it Riss. It's an anagram and the numbers add up. 'Astral Glory MVP Ox. The numbers add up to 143 or the code for I love you," I said.

Larisa turned and smiled to Amrita. "Astral Glory MVP Ox. He was talking about the golden days of Taurus. You are all so flushed with Egyptian symbology, this was the time of those people. Also the numbers equal I love you," Larisa said.

Amrita smiled then her smile was gone. She sat up.

"Who are you really?" She asked.

"I'm here for the Pindar," Larisa said.

"After there will come from the outermost countries, a German Prince, upon the golden throne; the servitude and waters met, the lady serves, her time is no longer adorned," Amrita said.

"She's talking Nostradamus Larisa. That's one of his quatrains," Eli said.

"So what you're basically saying is that Labac Hamashiach Morgenstern is the new leader, and he's making the Pindar insignificant? Is this a rebellion?" Larisa asked.

The look on Amritas face when she asked that was priceless. Jaw dropped. All sexuality gone.

"How did you know that?" She asked.

"Because I just do," Larisa said.

"Some of those most lettered in the celestial facts will be condemned by illiterate princes; punished by edict, hunted, like criminals, and put to death wherever they will be found," Amrita said.

"I understand. What's the game plan Amrita?" Larisa asked.

"Hey guys, get a look at this that Baba just drew. Does it mean anything to any of you?" Rosette asked as she showed us a picture.

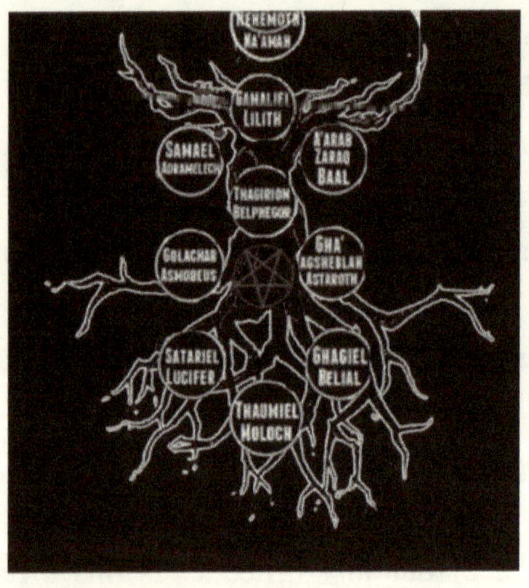

"That's the symbol of the Tree of Death. It's found below the Tree of Life which is Kabbalistic and esoteric in nature. What did she say about it?" Eli asked as he put his glasses back on.

"Oh my God," Larisa said as she turned around so that Amrita couldn't hear her.

"What is it?" I asked.

Larisa swiveled around and made her way back to Amrita. She pushed her down on the bed and laid on top of her again. She then softly planted a kiss on her lips. Amrita was in ecstasy. Then Larisa started making her way down to her crotch again, but this time she grabbed her left leg and put it down on the bed. We all saw the same thing. This was the tattoo that Amrita had on her calf. Amrita was the Pindar.

The study of the occult arts is not devil worship! It is self-worship of your own oneness with ALL and a celebration of being awakened to life beyond modern day matrix of ignorance. —Initiate of Luxor

Chapter Nine

Thirty minutes ago

"Guys I'm going dark. I need to work on this girl. Ciao!" Rosette said as she pulled her earpiece out of her ear. She turned to the young girl and smiled.

"Who am I talking to right now?" Rosette asked.

"It's Venga. I'm here. So, what are we doing here? You gunna fix me or something?" She said as she laughed.

"Nothing like that. I just need some information in helping find who we're looking for. I don't suppose you know who the Pindar is?" Rosette asked.

"Ha, even if I did, why would I want to help you guys. You don't care about us at all. You just run all over the world, not caring who you hurt along the way," Venga said.

"That's not true at all. Without us, without Graham, the World would have collapsed a bunch of times by now. No, we're the good guys Venga," Rosette said.

"If you say so," Venga replied.

"Tell me, when did you start protecting Baba?" Rosette asked as she crossed her legs.

"You're going to psychoanalyze me now? This ought to be great stuff for Graham's next book." Venga laughed.

Rosette leaned in. "You might not believe it, I'm not even sure if I would if I were in your shoes, but we are here to help you. Pease let me in, give me a chance," Rosette asked.

A long uncomfortable moment passed until Venga's body language changed completely. The girl in front of Rosette began scratching her head, then twirling her hair and after a few twirls, she would yank it out of her head.

"Hi Baba," Rosette said.

"Who are you? Where am I?" She replied.

"You're safe right now with some friends. Venga came with us. We're here to help you," Rosette said.

"Nobody can help me. My daddy is too strong. Him and some of his friends have something very bad planned coming up. I don't know what it is, but I know that it will destroy the world," she said.

"Baba," Rosette began as she took her hand and began rubbing her wrist slowly and methodically, "We need your help. I need to find the Pindar," Rosette said.

Baba just looked over at her and took the pen and pad out of her hand that she was using to take notes. She started drawing something, though she couldn't see.

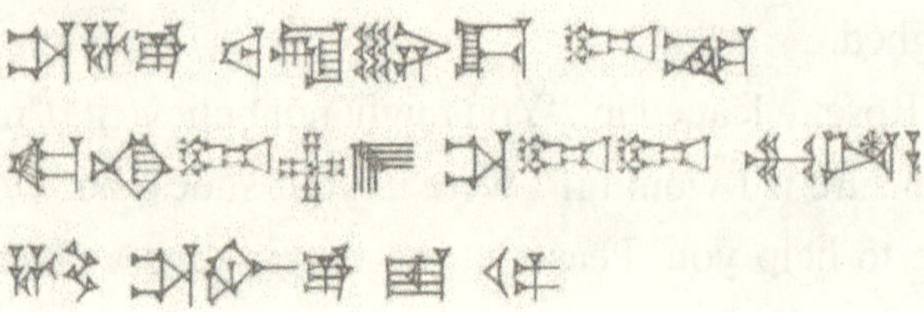

"What is this?" Rosette asked.

Baba shrugged her shoulders. "It's the last thing I remember seeing," she said.

"Do you mind holding on a minute?" Rosette asked.

Baba nodded.

Rosette got out of the car with the drawing and knocked on the other car. Josh opened the door.

"Eli, do you have any idea what this is?" Rosette asked.

"Where did you get this?" He asked.

"The girl drew this for me. I need to know what it is," Rosette said. "Please hurry," as she shut the door and went back in the other car.

"Whew, I thought you abandoned us for a second. Wouldn't be the first time somebody's tried to help us," Venga said.

"What happened to Baba?" Rosette asked.

"That's enough for her for now. What did she tell you?" Venga asked.

"She drew a set of pictures. Said it was the last thing she remembered seeing," Rosette said.

"Interesting. So what now sweetie pie?" Venga asked.

"What can I do to show you that I'm a safe place?" Rosette asked.

Venga fidgeted around. Rosette could tell that made her uncomfortable.

"I suppose you could tell us why you need the Pindar. What does it serve you?" Venga said.

"Some very bad men are trying to destroy the world and may have found a way to do so. We need the Pindar because she may be our only hope to lead us to them," Rosette said.

"I see. Well, I don't know who she is unfortunately, but Baba might. If I let her back out, you have to promise me that you will keep us safe," Venga said.

"I promise we will keep you safe," Rosette said.

Venga smiled and closed her eyes. Her eyes stayed shut for about two minutes, then like clockwork, her body language began to change, and Baba started with the hair pulling again.

"Sweetie it's ok, you're safe here with me. Venga let me talk to you again," Rosette said.

"She protects me when daddy gets drunk," Baba said.

"I'm so sorry about that," Rosette said.

Baba smiled. "I like you. You're nice to me," she said.

Rosette smiled. In her mind she pinned this girl's emotional development stunted at about 6-8 years old. That must be when the abuse started. So sad, Rosette thought.

"Can you tell me who the Pindar is?" Rosette asked.

Baba became incredibly uncomfortable. "She was very nice to me growing up. She always told me I was pretty, that I was special. Then something changed and daddy got elected. Now she's very scared because he said there were some new changes coming and she wasn't in charge anymore," she said.

"In charge of what?" Rosette asked.

Baba leaned in and appeared to look Rosette in the eyes. "Everything," she said.

"What do you mean everything?" Rosette asked.

Baba slumped back in the seat in the car and started stimming in the air. "I'd like to go back to sleep now," she said.

"Wait. Listen Baba, I think that I can help you. I'd like to try one last thing with you if that's ok," Rosette said.

"What?" Baba asked.

"I want to put you to sleep, not forever and not for real, like a pretend sleep. A sleep where you can help me out. If you help me, then I can help you out. Does that sound like a good idea?" Rosette asked.

Baba nodded her head.

Rosette took out her cell phone and put on the metronome app. It started ticking back and forth slowly.

"All right Baba, I want you to focus on my voice. I'm going to count backwards from 10. Each time I count, your eyes are going to get heavier and heavier. When I get to one and snap my fingers you are going to be asleep," Rosette said.

Baba smiled. "I like sleeping. It doesn't hurt when I'm asleep," she said.

Rosette shook her head. The trauma this girl has been through.

"All right, 10, 9, 8, your eyes are getting heavier, 7,6,5, they're even heavier now, 4,3,2, you're falling into a deep restful sleep and one," Rosette said as she snapped her fingers.

Baba's head slumped down.

"How do you feel?" Rosette asked.

Baba slowly raised her head and looked at Rosette in the eyes. "You're very beautiful," she said.

Rosette sat back slightly shocked. She didn't think that she'd be able to see once under hypnosis. Her hypothesis was that she was suffering from conversion disorder, but it was only verified now.

"Baba, I need your help. There's a woman that can help me and my friends. All we know is that she's called the Pindar. I know that you know her. Can you describe her for me?" Rosette asked.

Baba sat for a moment and took a deep breath and exhaled. "I can't show you because we are not back with everybody," she said. Even her cadence and vocabulary changed while she was under. This must be her true form.

"That's alright, is there anything that we can look for that can help us find her?" Rosette asked.

That's when Baba took the pen and the paper from Rosette again and drew the following.

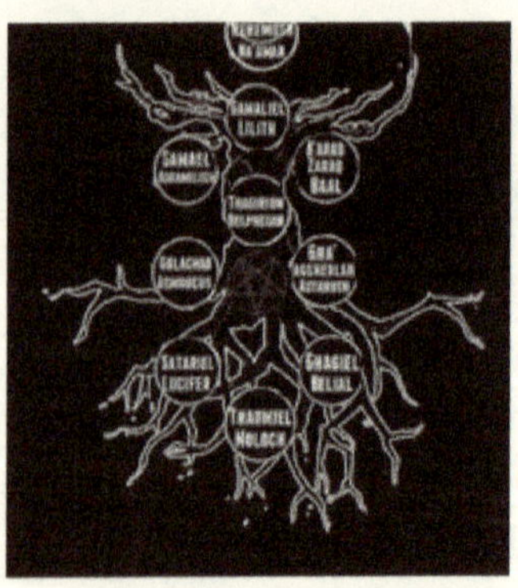

"Baba, what is that?" Rosette asked.

“That’s how you find her,” Baba said.

Just then there was a knock on the car door and Josh opened the door. His eyes were huge.

“Rose we figured it out. It’s ancient Sumerian,” Josh said.

Rose scratched her head. Was this glossolalia? She had only really put one person under hypnosis in her life and none with these particular set of issues.

“I’m in the middle of a session,” Rosette said as Baba started looking uncomfortable.

“I’m sorry. It says ‘The blind one knows too much. Her time is up,” Josh said. As he finished his last word Baba started crying and throwing a scene.

“Alright Baba, I’m counting back from 5. By the time I get to 1, you’ll be wide awake as if nothing happened. 5,4,3,2, and one!” She shouted as she snapped her fingers.

Baba opened her eyes and started looking around as if trying to see something. It was clear she was back.

“We have to help this girl. Why didn’t you tell me?” Rosette asked angrily.

“Because you were off comms. Also, we figured it was important,” Josh said as he shut the door.

“Baba, how are you doing?” Rosette asked.

“That’s enough for one day. I hope you got what you needed,” Venga said as she opened the car door stepped out, walked a few feet, squatted and peed.

This poor girl was going to end up dead. Her protector had no idea that her life was in danger. Rosette couldn’t worry about this now. She put her comms back in her ears.

“I’ve been speaking to this girl for a little bit. From what I can tell she’s got MPD, trichotillomania and something called conversion disorder. This would take a lifetime to undo, but I’m going to keep trying,” she said.

“In English please?” Josh said.

“Right, sorry. She’s got multiple personality disorder. From what I can gather it started when she was molested as a young kid. It also stunted her mental growth, which is why she talks like a kid. She also has a habit of pulling her hair out when she’s Baba. Venga came in as one of her personalities to protect Baba. I haven’t made much progress with Venga, but she’s allowing me to speak to Baba. Conversion disorder is a tricky thing to explain, but basically this girl is not blind. But for some reason she only presents blindness with her actual self. Venga can see perfectly well. I’ve been trying Erickson’s waking hypnosis to work on her. It’s basically hypnosis while you are still awake. You start by shaking their hand, in an awkward way, I can’t get into it right now.

Just know I'm working on this. How long until Larisa's back?

"I don't know. She's playing a cat and mouse game with this lady. As long as she doesn't try and do anything horrible, we'll just deal with it," I said.

"Alright, keep me posted," Rosette said.

Rosette sat in the seat for a few minutes going over everything that just happened. Then she remembered the drawing.

"Hey guys, get a look at this that Baba just drew. Does it mean anything to any of you?" Rosette asked.

There was a silence on the other end.

"Guys, I'm with her right now," Larisa said as she showed us the same drawing on this lady's leg.

The Atheist complains about the wind. The Christian prays for it to change. The Satanist adjusts his sails—Anton LaVay

Chapter Ten

"What are you doing to my leg darling?" Amrita asked.

Larisa's body language completely changed. "You're the Pindar," she said.

Amrita smiled then laughed.

"Someone figured out the tattoo. Congratulations. Hey, any chance I can get another one of those shots to my thigh?" Amrita asked.

"First you have to help us out," Larisa said.

"Well, I don't know how I can, being all naked with you," she said.

Larisa smiled.

"We have Morgenstern's daughter. She's been helping us out," Larisa said.

Amrita stopped and sat up, this set her sober for a moment.

"How is she doing? I didn't get a chance to talk to her when I met you guys by her place a little while ago. Is she doing alright?" She asked worried.

Larisa was confused. Here was a lady whose time was nearly up and she's worried about the daughter of a man who was after her.

"She's safe. One of our friends put her under hypnosis and she gave us everything we needed. Now we need your help. We can protect you," Larisa said.

Amrita laughed.

"Nobody can help me dear. Nobody helped me when I was knocked up, and nobody can help me now. It's like Labac has been telling everyone, I'm on limited time," she said.

"What do you mean knocked up?" Larisa asked.

Amrita stared out the open window. "It was almost 20 years ago, but I can still remember it like it was yesterday. We were here, Labac was just a 30-year-old, lost in the world. His cousin had brought him here to our ceremony and he fell in love with it immediately. He took to all the traditions, until the former head of operations here died, and he took over as interim. It was only supposed to be for a year or two." Amrita said as she sighed and trailed off. "We had a party, much like tonight's, and it went much like tonight went. At one point Labac ended up in my room, and I had just too much to drink that night. He spent the night with me. He didn't seem to mind that I was a few years older than him, in fact, I think he thought of it more as a conquest. 3

weeks later I was pregnant, a little girl. Labac was beside himself. He wanted to work his way up to total power, but he knew that he was going to have to indoctrinate her into our way. He ran away and hid for the remainder of the pregnancy. The people here didn't like that. When you're here, you're in it for life, and that's not always a long one. They found him and killed his entire family to teach him a lesson. Tied him up, hit him with cattle prods and water torture. A few months later, he was back to running things here. After about two years he knocked on the door to my house with some from this society and ransacked my house. They tied me up and took my baby. She calls herself Baba because that's all she could say when she was that age, but I had named her Brianna, after an actress that I liked and had once slept with. He's been raising her to this day. Seeing how she acts, how she has split personalities, I can only imagine the monstrous things he had done to her in order to keep the society happy." Amrita paused, getting angry. "If Brianna was comfortable enough with you to leave her post and give you that information, then I have to trust you as well. I just want my baby back," Amrita said.

"You do realize that you tried to kill us in the past right?" Larisa said.

Amrita shook her head. "If I wanted you dead, you would never be found, not with cadaver dogs. I let you live overseas. I could have come in and shot you all. It seems like nobody will just do that to you. You keep escaping everyone's grasps, it's really incredible you've made it this far," Amrita said.

"We were all shot in Minnesota. We just got lucky," Larisa said.

"The point is I will help you, but you've got to help me first," Amrita said as she turned around and dropped her dress.

"I'm sorry Amrita, but I'm engaged, I can't," Larisa said.

"Woo hoo!" Jean said.

"Shut up Jean," Rosette said.

"No child, I need your help. I have a tracking device on me. Call it the mark of the beast if you will. If I go anywhere out of the ordinary, they will hunt me down and kill me and possibly my daughter," she said.

"Your daughter's life is already in danger. She gave us a message in Sumerian that I can only admit she pulled from her father. It really is now or never," Larisa said.

"OK, but please help," Amrita said.

Larisa put down her glasses on the table and pulled out a knife from the desk. It seemed that people here had a knack for drawing blood. Amrita sat on the chair and Larisa stood behind her. Amrita pointed at the location.

"Uh, Graham you there?" Larisa asked.

"What's up?" I replied.

"Where are you?" She asked.

"I'm right downstairs hiding in the bushes like a creeper. Why," I replied.

"This is too close to her spine. It's one of the C vertebrae. I'm going to need you up here to remove this," Larisa said.

"Why me?" I asked.

"You went to med school," she replied

"I wasn't in long enough to do this," I said.

"Babe, I can't do this. I need you, just come up here," she replied.

"Alright," I said.

I crept out of the bushes and started walking up the stairs. I got to the room. The room smelled like a mix of pheromones and sweat, mixed in with some iron from the blood. Then I was finally face to face with the Pindar.

"Graham, you look so different," she said.

"Less people recognize me this way. It's a blessing and a curse. Let me see," I said as I looked at her back.

Larisa was right. I could see it, but it was wedged in her C2. It was going to take a little finesse.

"I need you to lie down on the floor and stay perfectly still. I mean perfectly," I said to Amrita.

"OK," she said as she got up from the chair and turned to me. She had an incredibly good body on her for being 50ish. She was pretty, but you could tell that her face had seen a thousand wars. She lay down on the floor with her arms up, face down.

"I need you to put your arms down to your side," I said.

She put her arms down. I had a good look at this thing now.

I sat down next to her and put one hand on her head to stabilize it. This was going to hurt like a motherbitch.

"Larisa, pass me the Zippo," I said.

She got it for me and handed it over.

"What are you doing right now?" Amrita asked.

"Sterilizing the knife. Here, bite down on this," I said as I tossed her a face cloth from the other chair next to me. At this point I couldn't care less if it was someone's old cum rag, I just needed her muffled.

"Alright on three. One, two," I said as I skipped three.

I very carefully went in directly. If I touched her nerves, she could have been paralyzed from the neck down. I had to be careful. All at once I heard a little muffled yelp from her as I dug in and popped the thing out. I caught it midair. I then lit the knife with the Zippo again and cauterized the hole I just made. She screamed into the rag.

"Alright we're all done. Can you wiggle your," before I could finish she popped up in the air.

"Larisa, can I get another one of those shots please?" She asked.

Larisa rolled her eyes and went into her bag. She pulled the pen that she had used before and walked over and jabbed it into Amrita's leg. She pushed the other half in.

All at once Amrita went from being completely in pain to completely ecstatic again. Her nipples got instantly hard, and she spun around.

"Alright guys, what say we get out of here," she said.

"Well, what are we going to do with this tracker?" I asked.

"If I leave it here, nobody will know for a little while, but eventually come and find I'm not here and they would know," she said.

"So what if we just throw it out?" Larisa asked.

"Same thing. They would track me down to a garbage can," she said.

"So what do we do?" Larisa asked.

We sat for a minute.

"I have an idea. Let's take it with us," I said.

"Are you nuts. Do you really want these people finding us?" Larisa asked.

"No, Graham's right. We bring it with us, then we put it in the back of someone's car. Let them chase it. By then we'll be off the west coast," she said.

"That's a good idea," Larisa said.

We walked down the stairs after Amrita put her clothes back on. We carefully made our way to the first building. On the bench there were discarded clothes and robes. Apparently, these people don't even wait to get in the building before they start the gangbang.

"Pick up a robe for each of us," I said to Amrita.

She walked over to the bench, pushed away all the other clothes and took 3 robes. She handed it to us, and we put them on. We started walking slowly out of the place like a bunch of monks. After a few minutes of walking, we came across some people still wearing robes.

"Hello brother and sisters," the first man said.

"What are you doing out here right now. Shouldn't you be having fun?" The other man asked.

"We like to do it by the pond," I said, distorting my voice again.

"Ah, by all means!" The first man said.

We made our way to the pond which wasn't that far from these two. They kept staring at us, so we all laid down on the grass together. Rosette took out a bottle of wine from her bag and unscrewed the cap. She took a big gulp out of it and then passed it to Amrita. She took a big gulp out of it as well.

"Aren't you having some?" Amrita asked.

"I don't drink anymore," I said. I almost felt like I could say that and mean it for the first time.

Just then, the men started walking back.

"Alright, now's our chance," Larisa said as she stood up and chucked the bottle into the pond.

We started walking back towards the cars again. After another 15 minutes or so, we were finally there. Everyone was there to meet us.

"I'm so glad you guys came out of this alive. Here, I have a surprise for you," Rosette said as she opened the car door.

"Mama?" Baba said.

"Hi baby," Amrita said, tears forming in her eyes.

We split up and got into the cars.

"How have you been sweetheart?" Amrita asked.

"Good mama. I want to play some songs for my friends," Baba said.

"She must really be comfortable with you guys if her other isn't out," Amrita said. She called her split her other.

Just then the car flooded with the Rolling Stones. We listened to it for a little bit.

"Why is this song important to you?" Rosette asked.

"Shhh. You'll see," Baba said.

We listened to three or four of them, then we listened to a few songs by Sly and the Family Stone.

"How do you know these songs?" Rosette asked.

We listened to a few more. Then I heard the first few chords of the next song.

"This is The Stone by Dave Matthews Band," I said.

I turned to Rosette.

"What is this girl doing?" I asked.

"I think she's trying to tell us something, but I have no idea what," Rosette said.

Amrita just sat in the back seat with her daughter, stroking her hair.

Just then the song ended. She started playing them from the beginning.

"What do these have in common?" I asked.

"Sweetie, did you hear daddy playing these songs?" Amrita asked.

Baba nodded her head. "They said that something very bad is going to happen that we won't be able to recover from. They said it all starts from the old hiding spot," Baba said.

Amrita turned to us and looked and shook her head. "I've never heard this in my life," she said.

"Old hiding spot?" Rosette asked.

"Yeah, and they said they left clues in case any of them were found out, others could complete the work," Baba said.

"Clues?" Rosette asked.

"Rose wait, the Stones, Family Stone, Dave's The Stone. What if this is a clue?" I asked.

She nodded. "Hey guys are you still on comms?" Rosette asked.

Yes's came in one by one.

"What do you think?" Rosette asked.

"I think it's brilliant," Josh said.

"What is?" I asked.

"Think about it. If you were going to kill someone and not get caught, the best way would be to call in a murder at a specific location. Then when the police get there and dig it up and find nothing, they wouldn't bother with it further. Then you bring the body in, the ground is already dug up, and you can just bury the body. Nobody would think to look there twice," Josh said.

"What does that have to do with this?" I asked.

"The Georgia Guidestones, Graham. The old hiding spot. They must have reburied a clue there, since nobody would think to look there," Josh said.

We all looked at each other. Then I looked over at Baba. She started giggling.

"Alright, first, let's get the hell out of California. We can't hide them at my place, that would be too suspicious. But Jean, you have plenty of space. Do you mind?" I asked.

"Non, c'est parfait," he said.

"Alright baby, we're going on a little road trip, ok?" Amrita said.

We drove our way out of the ditch and onto the road. Jackson set the pace as the car followed behind us. We were going straight to the airport, back to Boston and then back to Georgia. What I didn't consider was the kind of clue we would find once we got there.

The pathway to enlightenment is barred by the necessity of a passage through hell. That's why there is not a world full of enlightened people—Jordan Peterson.

Chapter Eleven

We returned the cars and boarded the plane.

"Hey guys, what are we doing with the tracking device?" Amrita asked.

"We're going to hold onto it for the perfect opportunity to ditch it. We're headed back to Boston. The truth is that they don't know who we are, so it wouldn't look out of place for you to be in a different state. Plus, Boston is a major port, we could end up sending it overseas," I said.

"Good call," Rosette said.

I turned and looked over at Jean. He seemed really sour from everything that happened with Larisa and Amrita. Amrita had noticed the look I gave him, and she got up and sat by him.

"I'm really happy that you are helping us out. I can't thank you enough," Amrita said to Jean.

"No problem. It's not really your fault, it's just that every time we do something, Larisa ends up either half naked or on top of someone," Jean said.

"I'm really sorry Jean. It wasn't personal. You have to understand the lock and key they kept me under, the only things that I had under my control were drugs or sex. Larisa is a very smart and beautiful girl. She also knows a lot about the cryptic way that we talk. I was high and beside myself. Now that I'm sober and have my daughter, I promise you don't have to worry about me," Amrita said.

"She didn't know all that stuff Amrita," Josh said.

"What do you mean?" Amrita asked.

Josh took his comms out of his ear and showed her. Larisa took hers out next and we all followed suit.

"Oh wow, you guys were all live with each other at the time?" She asked.

Josh nodded.

"I had no idea," she said.

"You literally heard me asking Graham to come upstairs to help take your tracker out," Larisa said.

"Yeah, I guess I was high and didn't put two and two together. I'm sorry," Amrita said.

She slumped back down in the chair. God knows what this poor girl has been through since her power had been stripped by Labac. The control he has over their daughter, all the evil things that he had done to her. A lifetime of knowing what flu or plague was coming next and who was going to suffer while they stayed bunkered away with their millions and billions having drug induced orgies. If I didn't know her at this point, I would have said to hell with her. But the truth was, that we actually needed her alive to help us out, to help us figure out what was going to happen next. I took a look at Hannah and realized that loving her was the closest thing I could feel to Amrita loving her daughter, and it probably wasn't as strong a feeling anyway. I empathized with Amrita.

"T minus five minutes guys. Strap in," the pilot said over the intercom.

"Get us the hell out of here please," Jean replied.

"You got it boss man," the reply came in.

After about a five-minute delay, we were wheels up.

"It feels so good to get out of here," Amrita said.

"We're just glad your daughter is safe," Rosette replied.

The rest of the flight was uneventful. Aside from a little turbulence, it was a relatively normal 6-hour flight back to Boston.

We landed at Logan, and immediately got out and got into Jean's van from long term parking. We had to squeeze in because of the additional people now. It took us about an hour and fifteen minutes to get back to Jean's place at the Avalon.

We got out of the car and started walking inside. After about a five-minute walk, we were at his apartment.

"OK guys, welcome to our place," he said as he opened the door.

I had never seen an apartment like this. So big, everything new and elegant. He gave us a quick tour around the house and showed us Larisa's she shed, which looked like the server room at the radio gig I used to have.

"What do you do in here?" I asked.

"Work for Mayim, catch pedophiles on the side with Anonymous. You know the drill," she replied.

Jean had three bedrooms in this apartment. He walked Amrita over to the furthest room and showed her where she would be staying.

"You can use wifi here. This place is a safehouse, nobody would be able to find you," Larisa said.

"Thank you, I appreciate it," Amrita said.

"There is food in the kitchen, you can order in as well. Everything you need is right here. There's a gym downstairs, there's a balcony outside, there's an ATM downstairs." Jean said as he handed her a spare key he had.

"I can't thank you all enough," Amrita said. "Actually, I'm going to use the ATM downstairs. I have a hidden account that nobody knows about under a different name that has a few million in it. I'll just take as I need," she said.

"Alright guys, so are we ready to go back to the stones? Jean asked.

"Might as well," Jackson said.

"We did this once, we can do it again," I replied.

"How soon can the plane be ready again?" Hannah asked.

"It'll take about 2 hours to refuel and do a complete check," Jean said.

"Go make the call baby," Larisa said.

"Ok." Jean replied as he whipped out his cell phone and walked away.

"The Georgia Guidestones are being portrayed by the media as being a failsafe in case of a catastrophe. That's not the case at all," Eli said.

"I know Eli, we've already figured that out. The question is, are we going to be found out if we go there," I said.

"What about the tracking device?" Amrita asked.

"Hmm, good point. I think that we'll bring it with us. If it shows that you're in Boston for all this time they will probably just come for you." I said as I took it and pulled out my wallet. It had a coin purse attached to it. I unzipped it and put it in there.

"Don't forget it's there. I used to forget it was on me," Amrita said.

We said our goodbye's as Larisa grabbed her laptop and got back in the van. We hopped on the highway.

"Do you think they'll be ok?" I asked Rosette.

"Her other personality isn't going to just go away, but the more she's with her mother, the more she'll revert back to her childish personality. In that way her mother can have the relationship she never had with her growing up," Rosette said.

"When did you know you wanted to be a psychologist?" Jean asked.

Rosette paused for a moment. "I guess you could say it was in high school. My mom was schizoaffective, and we had a perfect relationship when she wasn't hallucinating or in mania. I always thought that if I could just learn enough about psychology, I could help her. It never worked out that way, but I've always wanted to help people. It's the same reason Graham went into Medical School, why NP went to the Zip Code Bandits even though his IQ was through the roof. At the end of the day, we all just want to help people," Rosette said.

I nodded and gave her a hug.

Just then a car behind us slammed into the back of us.

"What the fuck?" Jean asked.

The car behind us honked loudly a few times then did it again.

"Guys, what are we going to do?" I asked.

"I say we pull over and I'll beat the piss out of them," Jackson said.

"They could have guns baby. Relax," Rosette said.

We dealt with this for a few minutes on the highway. There was no place to pull over and nothing to do but keep being abused by this car.

Finally a man stood up through the sunroof of the other car with a megaphone.

"PULL OVER IF YOU WANT TO LIVE," the man said.

A chill ran up my spine.

"What are we going to do?" Hannah asked.

Just then a cop threw his wailers on and started chasing us. The car behind us stopped their shenanigans and tailed back. The cop rode past the other car and came up behind us.

"PULL OVER!" the cop said from the megaphone.

The other car sped away as we pulled over. Why was this cop pulling us over? We didn't do anything wrong.

Jean pulled over and turned the car off, rolled the windows down, put the keys on the roof. The cop sauntered over to us.

"Do you have any idea how illegal what you just did was?" He said off to the side.

"I'm sorry officer, but we were being chased by someone, I honestly have no clue what you're talking about?" Jean said.

Just then he came into frame, and I saw him.

"Holy crap. It's Kurt Wolfgang guys. We go back to High School. How did you find us?" I asked.

"One of you brilliant people a few miles back hacked a billboard and put a message on it saying that a van with this license plate was carrying drugs," he said.

We all turned to Larisa. I cocked my head at her and she just shrugged her shoulders.

"I'm assuming there's no drugs in here," Kurt asked.

"No, but we were being chased by a car," I said.

"I know, we have their license plate and are tracking them down. We saw what was going on and we pulled you over to let them think they got away. Also, to keep you safe. The APB came back on that vehicle, and it belonged to a hitman that was just released from jail," Kurt said.

A hitman? Was it possible that they knew we were hiding the Pindar I thought?

"Anyway, how you doing Graham? I see you're keeping busy on the internet, with your books, I heard they're making movies out of them. Almost didn't recognize you with that beard and shaved head," Kurt said.

"Listen Kurt, do you think I could get your number, just in case we get in a jam?" I asked.

Kurt took his sunglasses off and looked at me. "You're up to something again. Right now, aren't you?" He asked.

I nodded.

"I don't want to know about it right now, but for sure," he said.

We swapped numbers.

"Do you happen to know Officer Hitchlords?" I asked.

"Yeah vaguely. We met at a party a few years back. I'm actually going to be seeing him this weekend for a common friend's wedding," Kurt said.

"Would you say hi to him for me? For us?" I asked.

"No problem Graham. Where are you headed now?" Kurt asked.

"We're going to the airport," I said.

"Do you want an escort there?" Kurt asked.

"That would be great," I said.

"Alright then." He said as he slapped the roof of the car then tossed Jean the keys. "And quit hacking bill-boards. You're not allowed to do that." He said as he laughed and walked back to his truck.

We sat there in silence for a minute, the adrenaline still coursing through our blood.

"Is this the feeling that these elite's chase?" Rosette asked as she put her finger to her pulse.

"I suppose so," Jackson said.

Jean put on his hazards, and we followed Kurt to the airport. He gave us a salute as he made a 3-point turn and took off.

"Alright guys, are you ready for Atlanta?" Jean asked.

"I don't know what I'm ready for anymore," I said.

We boarded the plane and it shut its door behind us. We sat in our seats patiently waiting. The plane took off and I fell asleep.

"Every religion in the world that has destroyed people is based on love—Anton LaVey

Chapter Twelve

"Where is my daughter!" Labac screamed at his people.

"We don't know sir, but it seems that Amrita is missing as well," a response came in from one of the heavyweights in the room.

"I want them found. We have all the signs in order from the Gods to proceed," Labac said.

"Yessir Grandmaster," another man said.

"Well, what are you waiting for? Go!" Labac ordered.

Everybody scrambled out of the room.

Labac sat down in his favorite chair and took out a very fresh Cuban cigar. Ever since the World decided to come together as one and the Consortium was created, he was elevated to the top. It didn't come without a sacrifice though. He still had nightmares about his family being slaughtered in front of his eyes, but as comes with the job. You have to make a sacrifice in order to get to the level of power that he was at, and he didn't take that lightly. He had a strong grip on things and people feared him more than they liked him. He clipped the head off the cigar and lit it up with a Zippo that he found in Amrita's room. He placed it on his desk. He looked at his watch. It was three days until a massive explosion would rock Norway and decimate all chances of saving humanity. From there, FEMA camps would be instituted in the United States, and Halliburton was busy building other camps across the world under the auspices of being given money for the war that was beginning with China. Ever since they unleashed that virus on the World, Labac had been furious with them. He knew he was in charge of pretty much everything, but he had to wait for the signs. Those were the rules, and without rules we are nothing but animals. He took a deep drag of his cigar and inhaled it. These were so good you don't just savor the taste in your mouth. He kept taking drags and after a few moments he was getting lightheaded. The nicotine was intense.

"Honey, can you come in here please. I'm in a mood, and I need my pipes cleaned," he said into the intercom.

"Be right in," the girl at the other end said.

He slunk back in his chair and undid his belt and unzipped his fly. He didn't even view people as people anymore. Just a means of opportunity and to use them as well. There were very few people he respected. His top soldier Beez was one of them.

"Hello Grandmaster. What can I do for you?" A pretty young German girl asked him.

He motioned for her to come over with two fingers and then pointed down at his crotch.

She walked over and tied her hair in a ponytail and started going to work.

Labac started thinking about all the places Amrita and Brianna could be. He opened his left draw over the head of this girl and took out a small syringe filled with blood and tied his arm off. He waited for a vein to pop up, and when it did, he plunged the syringe deep into his vein and filled himself with the blood.

All at once his heartbeat started to race, his face became flush with color, and he started to breathe heavily. Two seconds later his whole body shook, and he collapsed into his chair.

"That'll do darling," he said as he waived her off.

Labac had injected himself with a young man's blood. It's how he was able to stay as virulent as he had been, as he was getting up there in age. A lifetime of misery and power was all that would remain of him when he passed, and he knew it. Unfortunately, he wasn't able to cum anymore without a little rush of new blood. But, now that he wasn't thinking about that anymore, he got back to work.

“Where are we with finding them?” He asked through his intercom.

“Still working on it. It seems they are on a flight right now by the way it’s moving. Unfortunately, we don’t know where it’s going to as it’s not a major airline. My guess is that it’s a private flight,” a voice came back in.

Labac picked up his cigar, puffed on it a few times then slammed his fist down at the desk. “I want to know where they are. Both their times are up. Once we get rid of them, there will be no stopping us,” he said into the mic.

“Roger that sir,” a voice came back.

Labac sat at his desk and thought long and hard as to what it would mean if their plan came to fruition. There would be no way to recover if there was an apocalypse. Once word got out that Norway had a major attack, the World would be deflated, and everything would start to unravel.

“I want them found before the explosion,” Labac said as he put the intercom through the entire building.

“Yes sir,” a voice came back and said.

Little did Labac know that the zippo he took from Amrita’s room would be the key to how his daughter and baby’s mother would be able to survive them for a while.

And now it stands proven that Satan, or the Red Fiery Dragon, the 'Lord of Phosphorus,' and Lucifer, or 'Light-Bearer,' is in us. It is our mind. —Madame Blavatsky

Chapter Thirteen

"Um guys, you're going to want to see this," Larisa said as she was working on her laptop.

"What is it?" Josh asked.

"Um, the lighter that I accidentally left at the Big Heaven Room is streaming," she said.

"Get the hell out of here," I said as I pushed my way to the front to see.

What I saw disturbed me.

Larisa attached her projector to her computer and streamed it against the wall of the plane.

We watched for half an hour as Labac who we recognized right away started barking orders to find the Pindar and her daughter. That people would be tracking her tracker, and in tune, would be tracking us. We watched in horror as he called a young girl into the room to go down on him. The video ended with him putting the zippo in his pocket. From then on, everything was muffled.

"We have to let Amrita know right away," Jackson said.

"Wait, we should wait on this. We could use this to our advantage," Rosette said.

"How?" Jean asked.

"As long as he keeps the lighter on him, we'll always be one step ahead of him and figuring out what the end plan is," I said.

"Exactly," Rosette said.

"Alright guys we're making our descent into Atlanta. What are we doing with the tracker?" Jean asked.

"Leave it on the plane. We don't want them knowing where we're going," I said.

I took my Armani wallet out of my pocket and placed it in the back of the plane.

"Alright, we should be good now," I said.

We landed after circling around ATL for a few minutes. Every time we drop in altitude, my ears feel like they're going to explode. I tried everything. I tried chewing gum, yawning, everything but having a drink. Nothing. Hannah noticed I was wincing in pain.

"Is it your ears again?" She asked.

I nodded.

She took me into her chest and rubbed the back of my neck. That always made me feel better.

After a few minutes of readjusting, I felt better, and we got off the plane. We had a Lincoln Navigator waiting for us. We all piled in the car and Larisa took out her phone and put in the directions for the Guidestones. Her phone had a scrambler on it, so nobody would be able to get her data.

We made the familiar trip that we had made previously back to the Guidestones. We parked the car and got out. I went around the back of the car and took a piss. Mid piss I was summoned.

"Graham, you have to see this," Jackson said.

"What?" I asked as I zipped back up and made my way to the stones.

They looked unrecognizable. There was dirt and mud all over it and somebody had spray painted 'Fuck the NWO' all over it. I laughed. I don't know if it was because of my books or what, but these stones were completely trashed.

"Alright guys let's go back to basics," I said as I turned to Jackson. He went to the car and pulled out a shovel that we picked up on our way here.

Jackson started digging until we hit a box. He pulled the box out. It was a small one, clear, you could see through. There was a scroll in it, but it had a key lock on the box.

"Is the key down there Jax?" I asked.

He shook his head and then started digging again. After about 10 minutes of digging he finally stopped, covered in sweat. He took his button down shirt off.

"Sorry G man, nothing here. Any ideas?" He asked.

I sat there for a minute and looked at the stones for some clues. Nothing. I sat down and lit a cigarette.

"What do you think honey?" Hannah asked me.

"I think we're screwed," I said.

"Can't we just hammer off the lock?" Rosette asked.

"Not without destroying the box." Jackson said as he held onto it.

Just then I looked up. I knew something was bothering me.

"Those numbers that were there before, they're different now. And there's letters on them as well." I said as I walked around. I took my phone out and started writing down these numbers. For the life of me, I couldn't figure out the numbers, but I took a look at the letters.

MILBC

"What do you think that means baby?" Hannah asked me.

"I have no clue. I think it's," I stopped all at once. I rearranged the letters.

CLIMB

I showed it to everyone. Jackson rolled his eyes and tied his shirt around his waist. I got up to the first stone with the NWO message on it and hoisted him into the air. He jumped and caught the top with one hand. He then pulled himself up with one arm until his other arm could reach. Then he got on top.

"See anything up there Jax?" I asked.

"You're not going to believe this," Jackson said.

"Why, what do you see?" I asked.

"It's a giant bird," he said.

"What do you mean?" I asked.

"It's a giant Cardinal," he said.

"What do you mean? Like an actual bird?" Rosette asked.

Jackson paused a moment. "Do you see a large bird from where you stand?" He asked.

She shook her head.

"It's painted on this stone I'm standing on," he said. "Wait, there's something else. Something in its mouth."

"What is it?" I asked. This anticipation forced me to crack open my pack and light up another cigarette.

"It's a key!" He enthused.

"What do you mean a key?" Jean asked.

"Like a key. It's got to be the key for that box below," he said

Jackson grabbed it and yanked it off the bird's mouth.

Just as he did that, the stone started to spin on its axis.

"Whoa guys are you seeing this?" He asked.

"Get down baby!" Rosette yelled.

"I can't it's spinning," he said.

The stone started spinning faster and faster.

"You're going to have to jump," I yelled.

"No way man," he said.

"Either that or it's going to fling you off of it," I said.

"Alright," he said.

Jackson tucked down and sprung out in a dive. As he was about to hit the floor he tucked in and did a roll onto the ground. As soon as he got off the stone, it stopped spinning.

"Anybody have any clue what the hell that was all about?" He asked a little out of breath.

"Did it start spinning when you removed the key?" I asked.

He nodded.

"Then someone must know where we are or will know very shortly. Quick, give me the key," I said.

Jackson tossed the key to me, and I put it in the lock and turned it. It opened. I grabbed the scroll that was in it.

The bird of the dead. In the land that made it its own, where largest weeping willow is, the bird exalts these evil spirits. Circle

of salt alone protects and beneath the ruin is a map.

"What in the hell is that all about?" Josh asked.

"I have no idea, but let's get out of here before anymore weird nonsense happens," Jean said.

"I'm with him," Larisa said.

We got back in the car. We started driving down the highway and, after a noneventful trip, we were finally back at the airport. We boarded the plane with not a clue what to do with this riddle.

"Guys, we need to figure this out. These pilots are going to want OT pay, and we need to know where we're going next," Jean said.

"Alright guys, what do you have?" I asked as I went to the back of the plane and picked up my wallet. Checked inside and the tracker was still there.

"The bird of the dead is the Cardinal. They say that when one lands near you, it means a dead relative has come to visit you. But why the bird to begin with?" Rosette asked.

"Weeping willows are generally considered weeds, by the way they grow. The largest one is in Virginia. Is that where we need to go?" Hannah asked.

"In the land that made it its own, the Cardinal has nothing to do with Virginia. Good try though, but it can't be it," Rosette said.

"Since when did you become a bird expert Rose?" Larisa asked.

"Since I saw your dove tattoo above your belly button back in that treehouse," she said and giggled.

Larisa blushed.

"I got Larisa to blush. That's a first. Points for me!" Rosette said.

"Yeah, yeah, don't forget who has your number sweet cheeks," Larisa said and winked at her.

Rosette burst out into laughter.

"I'm glad you guys are having fun here, but we need to get a snap on this," I said.

"Alright, sorry." Larisa and Rosette said in unison. Then turned to each other and giggled again.

"Anybody with any ideas?" Jean asked.

We sat there for about an hour and a half trying to figure this out. Then out of nowhere we heard a clank. Then another clank. Then a small barrage of them. I looked out the window.

"Guys, we're getting shot at here," I said.

"WHAT?!" Jean asked as he ran to the pilots to tell them to take off,

"Where are we going?" One of them asked.

"Back to Boston for now! You see those guys to the left of us?" He asked.

"Oh crap!" He said. "Alright. Everybody in your seats," he said

After a brief delay, we were taxiing down the runway, trucks chasing us down the runway. At the last possible moment, the pilot pulled his control up and we were headed about 70 degrees in the air. At least that's what it felt like. Once in the air and stabilized, we looked around at each other.

"Alright guys, what the hell was that all about?" Jackson asked.

"Either this tracker gave us away and they found us, or you did something on your dancing bird platform before when you took the key out," I said.

"What do we do now?" Hannah asked, visibly shaken.

I unbuckled my belt and went over to comfort her.

"Jackson, what was that riddle again?" I asked.

"The bird of the dead. In the land that made it its own, where largest weeping willow is, the bird exalts these evil spirits. Circle of salt alone protects and beneath the ruin is a map," he said.

"Alright so the bird of the dead is the Cardinal. In the land that made it its own. Does the Cardinal mean anything to any specific place?" I asked.

"Well, you've got the Arizona Cardinals, the St. Louis Cardinals. The Arizona Cardinals are actually the oldest franchise in the NFL, going back to 1898. So, Phoenix or St. Louis? What would we be looking for there, exactly?" Jackson asked.

"I don't think it has to do with the sports franchises. In the land that made it its own. Larisa, can you check on your computer if the Cardinal means anything to any of the states?" I asked.

"On it," Larisa said.

"Has anybody realized yet that we literally have no idea what we're looking for. We just know the World is going to explode," Rosette said.

"We're working on it Rose," I said.

"Newsdon, I love you as much as the next person, but after I take this panic dump that I've been holding in since we were shot at, we're going to have some words," she said as she unbuckled her seatbelt and walked in the back to the bathroom.

"Such a classy lady my girl is," Jackson said.

"Got something, but not sure if it's what you're looking for," Larisa said.

"What do you have darling?" I asked.

"So apparently Indiana's state bird is the Cardinal. Thing is, I can't find anything about the weeping willow. I found something," she said.

"What is it?" I asked.

"This has to be it Graham," she said.

"Don't keep me in suspense. Truth is, I might have to use the bathroom soon myself so give me the news," I said.

"It's not weeping willows, but this is a house in Indiana called Willows Weep. It says here all kinds of crazy things," Larisa said.

"Like what?" Jackson asked.

"Like basically it's built to look like an upside down cross. Also, that it's the most haunted house in the entire United States," she continued.

"The inverted cross…" Eli began.

"We know, we know. Cross of St. Peter. Got it. But to these people, they take Satanism seriously as a legitimate being and belief system. We can't be too careful. What's the circle of salt?" I asked.

"Circle of salt protects you from evil spirits. Salt was once the most precious commodity on the planet, to own it meant wealth. It has the same effect as garlic on vampires to put it crudely," Eli said.

We all looked at him.

"Well, why didn't you say something until just now?" Jackson asked.

"I didn't think about it at the time," Eli said.

I turned back around to everyone. "Alright guys, well if we're going to Indiana, two things are going to be for sure. First, we're getting rid of this tracking device. Second, we don't know what we're going to find there. Where is this place anyway?" I asked Larisa.

"Cayuga. It's 94 miles away from Indianapolis International Airport," she said.

"Exactly and if these people who were shooting at us were part of a bigger deal or part of Labac's crew, they'll be waiting there for us. No. Chicago is only 50 miles further. Jean, please tell the pilot to take us to Midway International Airport," I said.

"Why not O'Hare?" Rosette asked as she sat back down.

"Just in case they're waiting there too," I said.

"What was the second thing?" Eli asked.

"Huh?" I said.

"The second thing. You said there were two things. What was the second thing?" Eli asked.

"We don't know who's going to be at this house. We may have to bring something. We don't have any weapons. Maybe we can stop off at a gun store in Chicago," I said.

Jackson giggled.

"What's so funny?" I asked.

"Buying a gun in Chicago? Good luck," he said.

"Do you have any bright ideas? I asked.

"I do," Larisa said as she went in the back and came back with a gun.

"What is this?" I asked.

"It's a gun Graham," Larisa said.

"It looks like a freaking nerf gun," I said.

"Shut up. It's the first gun I've ever owned. Can't ever be too careful with the work I'm in now," she said.

"Well, I hope we don't need to use it," I said.

"Don't worry, I have something else in case that doesn't work," Larisa said as she pointed to a jar in the back.

"What would be in that darling?" Rosette asked.

"You can't handle it girl, don't tempt me," Larisa said.

Rosette giggled.

"Jean, what's our ETA to Chicago?" I asked.

"About another hour and a half," he said.

"Good," I said.

I closed my eyes and tried to catch a quick nap. Running around the US gets exhausting. Little did we know not only were we being tracked, but we definitely pissed off the wrong people.

Science is always discovering odd scraps of magical wisdom and making a tremendous fuss about its cleverness—Aleister Crowley

Chapter Fourteen

"Grandmaster, she got away," a voice said to Labac through the phone.

"What do you mean she got away?" Labac's voice thundered into the phone.

"Sir, I'm sorry, but the plane took off before we were able to make our move," the voice said.

"Where is she headed now?" Labac asked.

"From what we can tell, she's going to Chicago," the voice said.

"I want a team waiting for her at O'Hare. If she's not with my daughter, I want her tortured until she gives it up. Then just waste her," Labac said.

"Roger that sir. I'll send a team," the voice said as he hung up.

Labac slammed the phone down on the receiver, then turned and threw all his paperwork on his desk onto the floor. He fumbled around in his inner suit pocket for a moment and took out a cigar. He bit the tip this time and spit it into the garbage can. He then took out his zippo and lit the cigar, placing the zippo on the desk. He sat back down in his chair, exhausted from being up for two days of cocaine and prostitutes. He wiped the sweat from his brow, as he contemplated his next move.

"Beez, will you come in her a moment," Labac said to the intercom.

"On my way," a voice replied.

After a few moments, a tall muscular man came into the room, looked at Labac and pulled up a chair.

"How are you Beez?" Labac asked.

"I'm fine I suppose. A little worried about you. You have an empire to run, and you're stuck worried about your ex sprucing around the United States. Why do you think there's something nefarious going on with her anyway?" Beez asked.

Labac turned to him as he ashed his cigar. "Because old friend, she has my daughter with her," Labac said.

Beez looked bewildered for a moment at Labac and then his face reset to normal. "Isn't she her daughter as well?" Beez asked.

"That's not the point. Anytime Bri goes anywhere, I have a team of people protecting her. Anytime Bri goes anywhere, I know about it. I'm worried about what they're doing," Labac said.

The truth was, Labac wasn't really worried about anything. He knew in the back of his head what he had, what his closest in the elites have done to her. He knew that he messed her up mentally to the point of having a split. The truth was, he didn't really care about his daughter at all. He just used her as leverage to get the Pindar out of power, which worked, or at least seemed to have been working until now. He must find them and dole out appropriate punishments to both. No, Amrita wouldn't be allowed to see the light of day again, and his daughter, well, she was a blossoming end stage teenager at this point. To say that he had no shame or morals would be incorrect. Labac had a compass like each and every one of us, but power was most important to him, so he ignored it.

"Where were they last?" Beez asked.

"They were flying out of Atlanta. My team got there a few minutes too late and only were able to shoot at the plane. I always tell these dumbasses, take out the wheels, take out the wheels. But do they listen? No. Now they're on their way to Chicago," Labac said.

Beez sat back in his chair and took a look at Labac. He had always been there for him and done what he asked. Beez was aware of what they had done to Labac's child, but Labac never once asked him to participate. It seemed to Beez that Labac respected him enough to keep him out of that kind of mess. For that, Beez was grateful. He had always been a fan of Labac and watched him rise in the ranks years before. He was there for him when his family was killed as a sacrifice, and he is here for him now.

"Do you want me to go to Chicago to see this through?" Beez asked.

"That's very kind of you dear friend, but I need you here helping me out and backing me up. I've already sent a team to O'Hare to pick them up. Once they get back, I'll need your help to find out what they've been doing," Labac said.

"Then that is what I'll do for you," Beez said.

Labac grinned and then nodded his head. That usually signaled Beez to leave the room. Beez stood up and bowed to him.

Labac sat back in his chair. Conversations with Beez always had a way of making him feel better. He finished his cigar and snubbed it in the ashtray. He grabbed his balls, and lifted them up, and let them drop. Empty. No need to have them cleared out. He looked around as if looking for something to do. He threw on the TV and Blur Slanders was on. Labac's blood started to boil, and he turned the TV off and threw the remote. He removed another cigar from his pocket and lit it up. Blur was the one that infiltrated the Big Heaven Room and filmed a video of their rituals. This man infuriated Labac, but because he was so wild and unpredictable, and popular to boot, he was untouchable by Labac. There were very few people in the world that were untouchable. No, killing Blur would have severe consequences as the man regularly has 6 million listeners on his show every single day. Labac, now slightly frustrated, sat back and waited for some news from Chicago. Little did he know that his child and her mother were having help. Also, that they weren't on that plane.

What is more absurd and more impious than to attribute the name of Lucifer to the devil, that is, to personified evil. The intellectual Lucifer is the spirit of intelligence and love; it is the paraclete, it is the Holy Spirit, while the physical Lucifer is the great agent of universal magnetism—Eliphas Levi

Chapter Fifteen

We shut the livestream down as we were about to land in Chicago.

"Good call to not go to O'Hare," Jackson said.

"Yeah. So, Larisa, what's in that jar?" I asked.

"Don't worry about it, Graham," she said.

"Come on," I pleaded

"Alright. It's a penis extending cream," she said.

"What?!" Jean asked turning red.

"Yeah," she said.

We stopped and looked over at Jean. He shook his head no.

"Thank God, that is one problem I've never had to deal with," Jean said.

"I mean, I've gotten drunk and swallowed a handful of gas station Viagra before," I said.

Everybody looked at me.

"Look never mind. What's the plan?" I asked.

"Well, we have a car waiting for us at the airport. It should take 2-3 hours to get there, depending on the traffic," Jean said.

"Alright good. Is everybody ready to go?" I asked.

They all nodded.

"Good, let's get out of here," I said as we got off the plane.

The ride was uneventful for the first 30 minutes or so, until Josh and Eli started in with the Luciferianism again.

"Lucifer is the first-born primal force. He predates all of them. Everything negative towards him are because of two pieces of work. Dante's Inferno and Paradise Lost. The truth is, although never mentioned by name, he was one of the first mentioned. The first mention of Lucifer is Genesis Chapter 1 Line 3. The whole God said Light and there was Light. You can't have light without the light bringer," Eli said.

"Right, but it goes further back than that. The inspiration for Genesis is the Enuma Elish, The Sumerian Genesis. The Sumerian Identity was Mummu. Mummu starts an assassination attempt on the Gods, and then as Kingu leads a band of demons against them and loses to (B)El. There's even another version of the story. It's found in the Greek Cosmogonies. At the beginning of time there is Nyx (night) and Tartarus (the deep). Then a cosmic egg was formed, born of Necessity. Out of it came Phanes, one of the deities worshipped by Orphism, the firstborn deity born from the cosmic egg. As Lucifer is the first-born angel, he is also the first-born primal. A blonde hermaphroditic deity with a torch. Phanes was called Eros and Protogonos which means the first born. He was considered the same as Mithra and Sol. Mithra is where the word Miter comes from, the head covering of the Pope. Phanes means 'Bringer of the light' and from Greek to Latin and it becomes Lucifer. Mithra was born from a rock in the primal sea except for a torch in his left hand. Just as Phanes. Mithra is also a peaceful deity who despises all violence," Josh said.

"Right, exactly. Lucifer is not a new being, he's as old as time. He's a metaphor for being your best self. He is castigated because he tried to help humanity out by giving them knowledge. The Garden of Eden, the first part 'Lucifer' shows up comes from 4 different stories. Enki and Ninhursaga, the story of Adapa, Inanna and the Huluppu tree, and Inanna and Shakeltuda," Eli said.

"Wait, guys slow down. What are you saying exactly?" I asked.

"Just that Luciferianism and Satanism has been completely perverted by the Church since day one. It has killed off anyone who knew the truth, and kept people hidden in their Dogma since. The truth is, when you go to pray in a Church, Temple, or Mosque, they are keeping you at a low vibrational frequency. The key is to attain Christ Consciousness, which comes when one is completely enlightened, like Buddha was," Eli said.

"I'm guessing Satan ruling Hell and also being Lucifer isn't true?" I asked.

"The writings are all there if you're interested to read. It couldn't be further from the truth. Some understand this which is why they worship Lucifer. But many worship the deity without understanding that it's not a creature or person, but an idea," Eli said.

"Alright guys. So what's next?" Jean asked.

"Wait, pull over at that truck stop," I said.

"Why?" Jean asked.

"Because I have to pee," I said.

Jean drove around and pulled into the rest stop. I got out of the car, went behind it and took a quick piss.

"Hand me my wallet," I said to Rosette through the window.

She tossed it out the side of the car.

"Thanks," I said as I picked it off the floor. I dusted it off then walked over to a 53 footer that was parked. The man got out of the truck and went in, probably to use the bathroom or get a sandwich. I creeped up to the truck where there was a piece of duct tape on the back. I peeled the duct tape back and put the Pindar's tracker in it and sealed it up. I ran back to the car and got there just as the man was getting out.

"Let's just hope he's going cross country," I said. "Get us out of here Jean."

Jean drove another 2 hours while we were just shooting the breeze in the car. The more I learned about Luciferianism and Satanism I realized that I had been taught a lie from day one.

We pulled up to the house and got out. There was a beater that couldn't possibly work under the tree. We approached the car to take a look inside. There were some shotgun shells on the passenger side seat.

"This can't be good. Do you think someone's inside?" Hannah asked.

"Everything I've looked up says this house has no residents," Larisa said.

"Then why isn't it boarded up?" I asked.

Larisa shrugged her shoulders.

"Alright guys, we don't even know what we're looking for here. So, let's just be careful," I said.

"Wait. If there is someone in there with a shotgun, they might be a little more friendly if one or two people go. The rest should stay in the car," Larisa said.

"What do you suggest?" I asked.

"If there's any technology in there, I can handle it so I think I should go," Larisa said.

"Alright, I'll be behind you and have your back," Jackson said as he took the gun out of the trunk.

We all piled back into the car. Larisa had put on her glasses and her comms. We were able to stream her view on the front windshield. Jackson cut back and went around the side. The garage was wide open, but there was nothing in it. Larisa kept walking until she heard a loud gunshot. She yelped.

"What are you doing on my property young lady?" The man asked. "You're not one of them reporters, are you?"

"No sir, I'm not. I'm just lost and need to use the phone," she said.

The man looked her up and down and started to smile.

"What's in it for me?" The man asked.

"What?" She asked.

Larisa caught Jackson out of the corner of her eye about to shoot him but shook her head. He backed off into the darkness.

"Pretty little thing like you so far from home. I said, what's in it for me?" The man asked.

"What do you want?" She asked.

"What every man wants, he said as he licked his lips and stared at her breasts.

“Alright, can you just hold on for a minute, I have to run to my car,” Larisa said.

“Take your time sweetheart,” the man said.

Larisa came to the car and opened up the trunk.

“What are you doing Larisa. Jackson had a clear shot,” I said.

“If this man is guarding something and he winds up dead, they’re going to know we were here. Don’t worry guys, I got this,” she said as she fiddled around her bag. She smiled and pulled out a small container.

“Turn around Graham,” she said.

“What? Why?” I asked.

“Just do it,” she said.

We all turned around. After about 30 seconds she was done with whatever she was doing and walked back up to the man.

“Well?” The man asked.

“Well what?” Larisa asked.

“I’m not toying with you girl. I’ve got half a mind to put a bullet right in your head,” he said.

Larisa smiled at him and ripped her shirt open, exposing her breasts to him.

“God damn it. Why does this always have to go this way!” Jean yelled.

The man put his shotgun down and swept Larisa up in his arms and buried his face into her chest. Then pulled back up and put her down. He then turned around to take her in the house when he fell face first on the floor. Larisa kicked him twice to make sure he was out.

"Come on guys, I bought us some time," Larisa said.

"Larisa, what the hell did you do to this guy?" I asked bewildered.

"Do your tits do that to everyone?" Jackson asked as he laughed back into frame.

We all looked at Jean.

"Can't confirm," he said.

"Are you even safe to be around?" Josh asked.

"Relax guys it's an old Columbian trick," she said.

"You're going to have to explain," Hannah said as we all walked up to her and Jackson.

"It's called Scopolamine, also known as Devil's Breath. Poor Columbian girls would smear it on their chest before they went out looking for men. When the men would suck on their nipples, they would ingest it, and it would knock them out. They would rob them and get away. It doesn't get absorbed trans dermally, so I'm fine. Just need to take a hot shower when we get back on the plane," she said.

"So, all those times I fell asleep after sex, it was because you drugged me?" Jean asked.

"No, that happened because I'm just that good in bed," Larisa said as she winked at Rosette.

Rosette giggled.

"Can we go in the house now? How long is he going to be out?" I asked.

"I don't know, I smeared a lot on, so probably an hour or two," she said.

I shook my head as I led everybody into the garage. We made it to the door leading into the house. It was locked.

"Jackson if you would," I said.

"No problem," he said as he cracked his knuckles.

Jackson big booted the door and it flew open. A few crows outside started cawing. We walked into the living room to a strange sight.

There was absolutely no furniture in the house at all. Nothing. I checked upstairs, nothing. The main floor was completely carpeted, that was all.

"Is this a safe house?" Jackson asked.

"This is supposedly the most haunted house in America," I said.

"Fantastic." Hannah said as she crossed her arms. "So, what are we looking for exactly?" She asked.

"I don't know, but we don't have a lot of time. Split up guys," I said.

Half of us went upstairs and combed every angle, there was nothing. We went back downstairs.

"Do you guys have anything?" I asked.

"Unfortunately, no," Hannah said

I looked around the room for anything at all. This was frustrating. I lit up a cigarette and started stomping around the floor like an angry child. Until I heard that thump.

"What was that?" Josh asked.

"What was what? Rosette asked.

"That noise. Do that again Graham," Josh said.

I stomped my feet where I was standing, and I heard a thud.

"Guys, there's something under here." I said feeling excited again. "Here, help me get this carpet up," I said.

We looked around for something to lift the carpet up with but found nothing. Until Larisa remembered she had a swiss army knife in her bag. Jackson walked her back in case the guy woke up, and a minute or two later they were back.

Jackson took the knife and started cutting the carpet around my feet. Finally, he ripped the piece he cut off. There was a trap door.

"Help me open this big guy," I said to Jackson.

We both lifted it, and a pound of dust flew up into the air. We started violently coughing. After a few minutes, we settled down. Jackson went around the back and lifted it while the rest of us stood back. It was dark, but it wasn't deep. I put my hand in and felt something like a blueprint. I pulled it out and it was a map. I unraveled it and turned my phone into a flashlight so we could look at it.

It looked like an ancient map on papyrus scroll. It showed the entire World, but something was odd. There was a section of the map where Norway was supposed to be that was cut out.

"Hey guys, what do you make of this?" I asked.

"Not sure. Why Norway?" Rosette asked.

"Is there anything else down there?" Hannah asked.

I reached down again and fumbled around. Mostly dirt, until my hand hit another scroll. I pulled it out, dusted it off and unraveled it.

Since the earliest of civilizations, there has always been a struggle for people to avoid catastrophes.

Even when everything seems to be going well, civilizations have fallen to dust. If not that, then war endlessly ravages the lands. The old way of doing things is no longer applicable. This world is beyond doing anything for. We can no longer save it. Countries like the United States and Russia will always vehemently be at battle with one another. We need a global reset. We are

overpopulated and it was only a matter of time before our land would sink to the bottom of the ocean like Atlantis, unless we put a stop to it now. I've left you clues within this letter that will help you locate the area lovingly chosen as the beginning of the end. It's time to start from scratch, see what new arises.

This was always the end game for each secret society known to man. Let's burn this motherfucker.

"Guys, any idea what we're looking at here?" I asked.

"Are they going to start a war between Russia and the United States?" Larisa asked.

Just then we heard some grumbling from outside.

"We've got to go now guys," I said as I grabbed up the scrolls.

We went out the back of the house and crept back to the car. We filed in as quietly as we could. Jean put the car in drive, and just as he turned around, the man from before came out with a shotgun and blasted a hole through our back windshield.

"You son of a bitches better hide. They comin' for you," he said as Jean chirped the curb and took off down the road.

After we all calmed down, Larisa's phone started to vibrate. She opened it and her eyes grew wide.

"Guys, he's back," she said.

To the occultist, birth is death and death is an awakening. The mystics of ancient days taught that to be born into the physical world was to enter a tomb, for no other plane of nature is so unresponsive, so limited as the earth-world. Time and distance were prison bars chaining the soul to narrow environments. Heat and cold tormented the soul, age deprived it of its faculties, and man's life was but a preparation for death—Manly P Hall

Chapter Sixteen

"I hate cigars, I don't even know why I still smoke them," Labac said as he took the zippo and lit his cigar.

"You could always just quit, Beez said.

"I always have to have something in my mouth.," Labac said.

Beez looked him over. It jogged a memory of them being drunk on the devil's punch as he called it, and they had sex. It was a long time ago, but Beez knew that Labac couldn't go long without a man or a woman to satisfy him. In fact, he was coming up on that time again where he would need someone. It had been a day or two, and for Labac, that was a day too much.

"Where are we with my daughter?!" He asked as he slammed his hand down on the intercom.

"We're tracking them right now. Looks like they flew into Chicago but went to a smaller airport. We were so sure it was going to be at O'Hare, but it wasn't," the voice on the intercom said.

"Well, what about it now?" Labac asked.

"We sent a team there to get them, but they were gone by then. Then the tracker started moving. We're following them as we speak. They are in Michigan currently, going north," the voice said.

Labac took a long hard drag off his cigar and inhaled it. He held it in for a few seconds and then blew it out. "So, they want to cross the border, do they? Do we still have people at the border?" Labac asked.

"Yes sir. Actually, we have a team chasing them. They're about 40 miles behind. They have to stop eventually. Once they do, we'll take care of them," the voice said.

"I want them back here, ALIVE!" Labac shouted into the microphone.

"Understood sir," the voice said as he hung up.

Labac paced around his office for a few moments and stopped.

"Beez, would you join me for a drink?" Labac asked as he went to his main door and locked it from the inside.

This is how things started years ago Beez thought to himself. He slowly sauced his way over to Labac and brushed his long hair from the front of his face.

“Do you still have the Sambuca?” Beez asked.

“Do I still have the Sambuca. Ha,” Labac said as he opened his cabinet and produced a bottle of it. He then took two shot glasses and two straws and closed the cabinet. They went back to Labac’s desk, and Labac poured the shots. He then took his Zippo and lit the shots on fire. In unison, they put their straws to the bottom of the shot glass and sucked the shot up, fire and all.

“God that burns like a bitch,” Beez said.

“I miss this,” Labac said.

“We should do this more often,” Beez said as he motioned for Labac to fill up the shots again.

“I wish I could. But between running a secret empire and trying to kill my ex, I’m completely swamped,” Labac said.

“I understand,” Beez said as he took another shot. “What are you going to say to her when you find her?”

Labac thought it over for a moment and poured another shot. “I’m going to tell her that leaving was the stupidest thing she could have ever done and that she will never see her daughter again, right before I put a bullet in her chest,” he said.

"It is time for the New Order to take over, isn't it? She's held her reign long enough," Beez said.

They took a third shot. Labac was starting to feel a little buzz.

"Come closer to me Beez. Let's celebrate the night together," Labac said.

Beez blushed and nodded. They poured another shot.

Over the next 45 minutes, they finished nearly half the bottle. They were both drunk, but neither of them was trying to hide it well. Slowly the clothes started to come off.

"Maybe I should have you around more often old friend," Labac said.

Beez laughed and flung his hair back. He walked up to Labac and was about to give him a passionate kiss when Labac tried to hold himself up on the table but slipped and fell. His cigar and lighter fell a few feet away from him.

"Are you ok dearie?" Beez asked.

"I'm fine, just a little fall. Here, help me up," he asked as he reached out with one hand and grabbed his cigar and lighter with the other.

"Oh damn it, I've lost my cherry," Labac said.

"You've lost that a long time ago grandmaster," Beez said.

"Please don't call me that, I hate it when YOU call me that. No, my cigars cherry." Labac said as he lit his cigar and looked at his lighter. Something was off. Suddenly rage filled his mind and blood vessels started popping out of his increasingly red face.

"What is it old friend?" Beez asked.

"Look at this!" Labac screamed.

When the lighter fell, it dislocated the video mechanism. Just as clear as day he saw that his Zippo that he had been carrying around was in fact a mini video recorder that could livestream.

"So, Amrita wants to play games, does she?" Labac asked as he threw the lighter into the fireplace. "We'll see who has the last laugh."

"How much does she know about everything?" Beez asked.

"She's got to know everything. I'm sending the ghost team in. Tell them to stand down in Michigan. Her time, both of their times will end now," Labac said.

Beez, still drunk, slowly put his clothes back on and gave Labac a salute. Their sausage party was going to have to be put on hold. Beez shook his head knowing that they will never find these two ever again.

The world is not prepared yet to understand the philosophy of Occult Sciences—let them assure themselves first of all that there are beings in an invisible world, whether 'Spirits' of the dead or elementals; and that they are hidden powers in man, which are capable of making a God of him on Earth. —Madame Blavatsky

Chapter Seventeen

"Well," I said as we finished watching the video.

"We don't have eyes and ears anymore. What are we going to do?" Hannah asked.

"Relax, they're still chasing a ghost in Michigan remember," Jackson said

"You're right," Josh said.

"How far until the airport Jean?" I asked.

"About another 45 minutes mon ami," he said.

We sat there, each with our significant other and Josh and Eli.

"Hey guys, what was your first conversation about?" I asked Rosette.

"Me and Rider?" Rosette said.

"Yes," I replied.

"He was talking to me about how if Tesla's work was made public that he'd probably be working on the Dyson Sphere or the Bishop Ring by now. I was probably talking about something psychology related. It was a hot day outside in Chestnut Hill, so he took his button down shirt off and well, that was the end of that," Rosette said.

"What about you and Hannah?" Jackson asked.

I laughed.

"What's so funny?" Jackson asked.

"I texted her 'talk dirty to me baby', and she replied, 'go sit in your own shit'. I was hooked from there," I said.

Everybody laughed.

"What about you Jean?" I asked

"Sorry, malfunction. Having technical difficulties right now," he said.

"Oh," I said. "Wait did you just say . . ."

"I know what I said," he replied.

I turned to Larisa and cocked my head to the side, advising her to get in the front seat with him. She did.

"Jean baby, what's wrong?" She asked.

"It's just that every single time we go out or more specifically when you go out, you either end up naked or humping someone," Jean said.

"You probably think I'm a pretty big hoe right now. But let me ask you this. Do I ever act this way in public whether I'm drunk or not?" She asked him.

He shook his head.

"And every time I've gone the 'extra mile' so to speak, did it not get us what we needed?" She asked.

Again, he nodded.

"Baby I love you. You know it's not for your money, I'm doing fine myself. Nobody has been able to understand me the way you do or is as freaky as you are," she said.

"Come on Larisa," Rosette said.

"You'll get your turn too, just be patient doll," she said

Rosette giggled and blushed.

"I'm not going anywhere, and I'll always be here for you, for us, for our team as well," Larisa finished.

Jean began to smile.

"Do you feel better now baby?" She asked.

"Yes, thank you sweetie," he replied as he turned his head and gave her a quick kiss.

"Alright now it's your turn Josh and Eli," Larisa said.

Everybody laughed.

We talked for another half an hour and finally showed up at the airport. We left the car and boarded the plane.

"Wait, I think we should call Amrita and find out if she's doing ok," Jean said.

"Good idea," I said.

Jean whipped out his cell phone, put it on speaker and dialed his home number. It rang off the hook. Smart of Amrita not to pick up.

“Hi Amrita, this is Jean, the guy’s house you’re living in. If you’re there, can you pick . . .” he said. She picked up before he could finish.

“How are you guys doing? Are you on your way back soon?” Amrita asked.

“Shortly, we just need to figure out where we need to go. What about you?” I asked.

“I’ve exorcised a bit of money from a bank account nobody knows about, I just went in town to pick it up. We’re going to Costa Rica. I’ll start a new life for me and my daughter. I can’t thank you guys enough for everything you’ve done for us so far,” Amrita said.

“Alright, we’ll come home and take care of you guys, then we’ll figure out where we’re going to next.” Jean said as he hung up the phone. He then stood up from his chair and went to talk to his pilots.

“Alright guys, while we have some time, want to try and figure this out?” I asked.

“The flight will be about 3 and half hours,” Jean said as he came back.

“What did it say again?” Josh asked.

I grabbed the scroll and opened it up.

Since the earliest of civilizations, there has always been a struggle for people to avoid catastrophes.

Even when everything seems to be going well, civilizations have fallen to dust. If not that, then war endlessly ravages the lands. The old way of doing things is no longer applicable. This world is beyond doing anything for. We can no longer save it. Countries like the United States and Russia will always vehemently be at battle with one another. We need a global reset. We are overpopulated and it was only a matter of time before our land would sink to the bottom of the ocean like Atlantis, unless we put a stop to it now. I've left you clues within this letter that will help you locate the area lovingly chosen as the beginning of the end. It's time to start from scratch, see what new arises.

This was always the end game for each secret society known to man. Let's burn this motherfucker.

"Well, this is obviously a New World Order executive. Depopulation, staging a catastrophe, mentioning secret societies," Eli began.

“They mention both United States and Russia. Two of the biggest places on Earth, and we’re supposed to find something in either of them?” Larisa asked. “We’ve got nothing to go on.”

“What does it mean that civilizations struggle to avoid catastrophes? Does that mean like avoiding nuclear war or something?” Hannah asked.

“Look at how many civilizations are now under water. Atlantis, Lemuria, Mu for example. Also don’t forget about the ice age in the past, asteroids that barely miss us. Even if a civilization is peaceful, it still might not survive. Look at Pompeii. Yellowstone National Park is basically overdue for an eruption which would wipe out the entire United States. Wait, maybe it has something to do with Yellowstone?” I asked.

“I don’t think so. There’s nothing in here to suggest that,” Eli said.

“Well, what do you think Josh?” I asked.

He thought for a minute. Then it hit him. “Wait, let me look at the other scroll,”

I pulled it out and unraveled it.

“Guys, Norway is missing here. That must have something to do with it,” Hannah said.

We talked it over for a little while as our plane was about to go into descent. Once again, my ears popped, and I couldn’t really focus on anything. Hannah cradled my head in her arms until we landed, and the pain went away. I didn't like how this was happening to me. It was never a problem before. Maybe it has something to do with the medication that I'm on now.

We got out of the plane and into the Van. Jean started it up and we were on our way back home.

"So guys, what do you think about this. What's 'start from scratch?' " Rosette asked.

"It has to be something that Blur was talking about. He would talk about how all the elites have underground bunkers built to withstand a cataclysm. That all the wealthy people were stepping down from their CEO positions and cashing out their stocks. There is a storm a coming, he says," I said.

"What would be the purpose of starting from scratch?" Hannah asked.

"Overpopulation. Everything we've seen so far has been about overpopulation. The virus vaccine, the Guidestones, everything we've run into. They feel the World is too crowded and there's nothing they can do to stop it," I said.

"But we already know that you could fit every single person on Earth inside the Grand Canyon and most of the population surrounds the coastline. There's a ton of room in all the states for people to live comfortably. Not everyone has to live in Boston or Manhattan or LA," Larisa said.

"It's not sustainable. Sure, every person could have a house in Alaska, but that's not realistic. They created this false narrative that we are going to run out of everything as the population grows, but that's just not true. Now they fear it, so they're going to sabotage our chance of global continuance," I said.

We talked it over for a little while until we pulled up to our house. We all piled in, exhausted from such a long series of events. We all just passed out on the couch and in the bedrooms.

We woke up in the morning and grabbed breakfast at the IHOP.

"Hey guys, maybe we should try the Pindar again," Rosette suggested.

"Good idea," Jean said as he dialed his home number. After it went to voicemail, he started leaving another one, just like he did previously so the Pindar knew it was us. But nobody picked up the phone.

"She might have gone to the bank or out to eat downstairs in the restaurant. Don't worry about it," Larisa said.

We finished eating and made our way to the Van.

"Guys, I'm a little nervous about the Pindar. Can you take a ride with me back to our apartment?" He asked.

"Absolutely," I said.

"Me too, I'm stuffed, I can't do anything right now," Jackson said.

We took the ride back to Jean's apartment and parked the car. We got out and went to his building. We just had to tell the Pindar a couple of things.

Destruction is a form of creation—Graham Greene

Chapter Eighteen

7 hours ago

"We're honingin' on the vehicle now sir," a voice came through the speakerphone.

"I want them dead!" Labac screamed into the phone.

"Roger that," the voice said.

Labac paced around the room and took a cigar out of his pocket. He bit the tip off and spit it into the fire. He took a new lighter out of his desk. He held the lighter in his hand, and as his anger started to boil over, his fingers wrapped around the lighter until his hand started to shake. He then took a deep breath and released the lighter. He lit his cigar and called Beez back into the room. After a few minutes, Beez walked through the door.

"Beez, how are you good friend?" Labac asked.

"Couldn't be better now that I see that you're in a good mood," Beez said. "What's up?"

"Today is a glorious day. This is the day that my two problems will be out of my life and things can go back to normal for me," Labac said.

"Sir, the tracker led us to a truck stop. It says they're in this truck," the voice said.

"A truck? What kind of truck?" Labac asked.

"A 53 footer," the man said on the other line.

Labac rubbed his head confused and looked at Beez.

"Alright, very slowly approach the front of the truck. Leave me on speaker so I can hear," Labac said.

"Roger that," the man said.

The team walked up to the front of the truck and knocked on the door.

"Can I help you?" A man's voice came in through the speaker.

"We're looking for two women. You wouldn't happen to know where they are, do you?" The team leader asked.

"No sir, I just stopped here to take a dump," the man said.

"Well, you won't mind us having a little look in the cargo, would you?" The team leader said.

"No way guys, that's private property," the man said.

The team leader pulled out a 9mm and aimed it at him. "What about now?" He asked.

The trucker laughed and pulled out a 6 shooter. "Please hombre, put yours away. I'm telling you there ain't nothin' in the back over there," the trucker said.

The team leader looked around at his team and cocked his head to the side. The other two members went around the other side of the truck.

“Afraid I can’t do that old man. We have orders to retrieve the two women, and we’re not leaving here without them,” the team leader said

“What women? Ain’t nothin’ back there but boars head meat,” the trucker said still pointing his gun at the team leader.

“We’ll see about that,” the team leader said.

“What makes you think I have women back there. Do I look like a coyote to you boy?” The trucker asked angrily.

“They have a tracking device on them. The tracking device says that they are right here, where you are,” the team leader said.

“Well, your dang tracking thing is wrong. Now put down your gun before I exercise my second amendment rights on you,” the trucker said.

Just then, the passenger side door opened up and one of the other team members drew his gun and shot the trucker in the head. He was using a silencer, but they aren’t as quiet as they make them seem in the movies.

“Goddammit, why the hell did you do that?” The team leader asked.

“I thought that’s what you meant when you cocked your head,” the second member said.

"I wanted you to go in the back and open the cargo lift, you dumbass. Now I gotta clean this guy out to make it look like a robbery," the lead said.

"What's going on over there?" Labac asked.

"He shot him in the head boss," the leader said.

"Why would he do that? That's not what we do here boys," Labac said.

"I'm sorry!" The second man screamed into the speakerphone.

"Just open the truck," Labac said.

"Sure thing boss," the team leader said.

After searching the truck for a few minutes for a key, they finally found it in the front left pocket of the dead trucker. The second man tossed it to the team leader, and they all got out to the back of the truck.

"Remember guys, do them quick and easy. No pain, then let's get out of here," the team leader said as he opened the truck.

The truck opened, and all they could see from here to the end was packaged meat. It was a refrigerated truck of course, so if the girls were in there, they were probably freezing by now. The team jumped into the truck and started combing through everything, all 53 feet of it. At the end, they found nothing.

"Uh boss, you're going to want to hear this but you're not going to like this," the leader said.

"Let me guess, they're not in there?" Labac asked.

"No sir. The redneck trucker was right. This is just meat in here," the leader said.

"Tear the entire truck apart. Her tracker said she's there. Check under, check in the bins, check everything." Labac said frustratingly as he put them on mute.

"I can't get anything done right with these people, it's unbelievable. I've got so many other pressing things to do right now that I have to chase the whereabouts of two insignificants," Labac said.

"Try and cool down. Would you like a shot of Sambuca to calm your nerves?" Beez asked.

Labac thought about it. The thought of getting drunk and having sex was incredibly appealing to him right now. But even more so than that, he wanted his daughter and one night stand found.

"Sir, you're not going to believe this," the team leader said.

Labac took them off mute.

"Go on," Labac said.

"The tracker was under a piece of duct tape on the side of the truck. I repeat, the tracking device has been removed," the team leader said.

"SON OF A BITCH!" Labac screamed as he picked up a crystal trinket from his desk and threw it into the fire, shattering it into a million brilliant pieces.

"What do you want us to do right now?" The team leader asked.

"For now, put the body in the back of the truck. It's refrigerated and should keep from smelling, by that time you'll be gone," Labac said.

"No problem boss," the team leader said.

Labac scratched his head again and looked over at Beez. That tingling in his crotch was coming back again.

"You know what, break out the Sambuca," he said to Beez.

Just then as they were taking their first shot, a man burst into the room.

"Sir, you're going to want to hear this. We found the plane that they flew in on to that smaller airport in Chicago. They were long gone by then, but we were able to ID it. It checks out to a Jacques Solex," the man said.

Labac put the man on hold. "Why does that name sound so familiar?" He asked Beez as Beez was pouring them another shot.

"He's the head of the wealthy Solex family out of France," Beez said.

"Interesting," Labac said.

"It gets better than that sir. We have reason to believe that his son was the one that chartered the plane, Jean," the man said.

"What is that supposed to mean to me exactly?" Labac said.

"He is friends with Graham Newsdon," the man said.

Labac choked on his shot. His eyes started filling with water as fire entered his lungs. He bent over and dry heaved for a minute before recomposing himself.

"Are you telling me that Graham Newsdon is with my soon to be dead family?" Labac asked the man.

"It would appear to be so. What should we do?" The man asked.

Labac thought it over for a minute. Did they still have that old connect in Michigan, by the time they figured that out they would probably be gone. This couldn't have to do with the 'end game' could it?

Labac took the man off mute on the speaker. "It seems that our targets have a friend. I'm chartering you three a plane." Labac said as he looked at the tracker. "It seems that you're closest to Grand Rapids Airport. Make your way there after you clean up IMMEDIATELY. I want you in Boston and at Jean's house by morning. We'll send you the address when we get it," Labac said.

"Roger that, sir. Thank you," the man said.

Labac paced around the room, puffing on his cigar. He took another shot and thanked Beez for the alcohol, but his adrenaline was running, more so than when he takes the sacred juice. He was going to wait up all night to hear the results of what his ghost team found.

Death does not exist because it is existence describing nonexistence—Kierkegaard

Chapter Nineteen

Current time

"Did you guys know that the Treaty of Tripoli that John Adams signed states that 'The government of the United States of America is not in any sense founded on the Christian Religion?" I asked them as we walked towards Jean's door.

"You do realize that no matter how much stuff you uncover, there will still be a majority of the people who think it's Satanic and that you need help. From all religious people," Rosette said.

"I resent that," Eli said.

"Sorry, well, Satanic as it's known to the masses. Whatever," Rosette said.

"She is telling the truth mon ami. I'm afraid it's just a dog that won't hump," Jean said.

"It's hunt. A dog that won't hunt you crusty Frenchman," I said. "Besides, it would be nice to at least enlighten some people. Take Ben Shapiro for instance. He went on his podcast and said that Astrology is dumb. I think I need to go in his studio while he's live, take a week old 20-pound codfish and slap him across the chops with it."

Jackson laughed.

"A codfish? Really?" He asked.

"Not to hurt him, but just to show him. Honestly, after everything that we've been through, the things I've written books about, I can't for the life of me understand how people can't see that the world is ruled by Astrology," I said.

"Well, that doesn't matter right now. Let's just go inside," Jean said as he fumbled with his keys.

Jean opened the door wide and took a step in. He dropped his keys to the floor. All our jaws dropped. Hanging from the chandelier were the bodies of Amrita and her daughter. There was a pile of fresh feces on the floor under them.

"Oh my God, shut the door," Jean said.

Eli slammed the door behind us.

"Why is there crap on the floor under them?" Jean asked.

"When a body dies, it usually leaks whatever was in it as there are no more muscle contractions to keep it in. I'd say they have been dead only a few hours. Jean, get me a ladder so I can get them down," I said.

"I wouldn't do that if I were you," a voice from the bedroom said.

Three men came out of the bedroom, one of them pointing a gun at us.

"I must admit, removing her tracking device was incredibly ballsy of you. A C2 C3 excision. You could have paralyzed her. I looked you up, you used to be in Med School amongst all the other problems you've been causing us around the world," the man with the gun said.

"Who are you and what do you want?" Hannah asked.

"Ah, you must be the wife. It's so nice to meet you." The man said as he took his hat off and bowed to her before putting the hat back on. "We are some people who you shouldn't have pissed off. You can call me El," the man said.

"El like the God of olden days?" I asked.

The man took a step up closer to me until he was right in my face. "You're very smart kid, I honestly don't know how you've survived so far. No matter, that won't be a problem. We're leaving now and we'll leave you to clean up or explain the bodies. You're coming with me," the man said as he pointed to me.

"That's not happening," I said.

The man laughed then clocked me in the side of the face with the butt of the gun. "I wasn't asking you. You're coming with me and," he said as he scanned the room "You, the mason. You're coming too. The rest of you can stay."

"If we go with you, you'll leave them alone?" Josh asked.

"We're here for you both. But don't worry, you won't be coming back anytime soon," the man said as he laughed.

The man took out two zip ties and tied mine and Josh's hands behind our back, then put his coat over me to hide it. Another man did the same for Josh.

"Enjoy the ride guys. T minus 2 days before the fireworks," the man with the gun said as he led us out of the building.

We walked out of the building and to a giant unmarked van. The man opened the door and threw us in and slammed the door.

"What are we going to do now Graham?" Josh asked.

I fidgeted with my restraints, but the man had put them on too tightly. Truth was I was losing circulation. The more I relaxed my hands the better off I felt.

"I'll figure something out," I said.

We were in the car for a good half an hour when we stopped. We heard a rumbling outside of the car. The man with the gun opened the door and lead us into a room. It looked like one of Senna Ore's futuristic science rooms. My thoughts turned to Conrad and his team.

What would they do in a situation like this? Just then, I felt a sharp blow to the back of my head, and everything went dark.

I was out for what felt like a few hours. I awoke with a splitting headache, tied down to a dentist chair. I looked to my right and saw Josh the same, still unconscious. I have been in this situation more than I had ever hoped or intended to. I looked to my left and saw a machine that I'd never seen before.

"OK, it's good that you're awake, now we can finally start," a man said.

"Where am I?" I asked.

"Somewhere in a dungeon in West Roxbury," the man said.

I looked at him and blinked. I didn't think he'd actually answer the question.

"Just in case you're wondering why I told you this, it's because you're not going to make it out of here alive," the man said.

"I've heard that before," I said as I rolled over to my right. Josh was starting to stir. He would be up in a few minutes.

"I have to tell you Graham, you impress me. You really do. It is mind blowing that you've gotten this far. Now with the Pindar and her daughter out of the picture, we can spend some time to get to know each other," the man said.

"What's your name?" I asked.

"I work for someone very powerful. My name is not important. If you like though, you can call me master," he said.

"There's no way I'm doing that," I said.

The man laughed as he flicked the needle on the syringe.

"Just a little something to take the edge off," the man said.

He injected me with a syringe, and in a few minutes I was very sedated. I felt completely carefree, not a fear in thc world. Am I high?

"Graham, what's going on?" Josh asked.

It took what felt like 45 minutes to turn my head. When I looked at him, I just smiled.

"Damn it, you're high. What did you give my friend?" Josh asked the man.

"Don't worry, it'll wear off shortly. I just needed his biorhythm stabilized." The man said as he started putting electrodes all over my neck.

"What are you doing?" I asked.

The man stopped what he was doing and sat back. He took a leaf out of his pocket and began chewing on it.

"This stuff is very good for you. Would you like to try some Jeff?" The man asked, looking at Josh.

"My name is Josh," Josh said.

The man laughed, then started laughing harder.

"It's CAT Josh," I said.

"What's CAT?" He asked.

"It's a drug," I said.

After a minute, the man wiped his tears and went back to work. He stuffed the leaf back in his pocket and continued attaching electrodes to the other side of my neck.

"I don't suppose you want to tell me what you know so far do you?" The man asked.

I looked at him with a stone-cold face.

"Didn't think so. No problem, we'll get you talking," The man said as he started to whistle.

"What are you doing to me exactly?" I asked.

"I think it's best if I show you," the man said.

"Now, do you know where the bombs are?" The man asked as he looked at the computer screen.

I stayed silent. I didn't know anything about the bombs. I wasn't going to say anything.

"So, you don't know where the bombs are. That's a good start," the man said.

"I didn't say anything," I replied.

"You didn't have to. See Graham, when you speak inside your mind, small muscles in your throat mimic the formation of each word. NASA worked on a machine that would detect muscle movements in your throat and transcribe them to words. They eventually had to shut that down for lack of funding, but we had all the resources in the World to continue that." He said as he looked at the screen and paused for a minute. "Yes Graham, I can read your thoughts, and I'm definitely in your head. So, let's keep going shall we. Did the Pindar tell you anything about what you are looking for exactly?" He asked.

I stayed silent. I tried my best to think of anything but the word no, but it's that whole thought experiment. If I tell you not to think of an elephant, what's the first thing you think of.

"I see. Have you found the maps yet?" The man asked. "Ah so you have. You've been lying to me you naughty boy." The man said as he rubbed my shaved head. "Now, have you decoded the letter that came with it? No not yet. Well brilliant, then we are done here. We have nothing more to talk about. You have no more use for us," the man said as he ripped the electrodes from my throat.

"What do you mean no more use. What did you need from me? You have bombs planted that are going to ruin all life's chances on this planet. What could you possibly get out of that?" I asked.

"Graham, what you don't understand is that there are underground cities all over this world that you don't know about. They even have them in Antarctica too. Most will eventually die of starvation yes. It will be a horrible time for the above ground people. The rest of us will be doing just fine. It's all about population control, Graham. There's too many of you to control anymore. We need a reset button," the man said as he wheeled up an IV pole. This can't be good.

"48 hours until showtime. Unfortunately, you won't be here Graham," the man said as he hooked me up to an IV.

"What is this?" I asked.

"I have direct orders from Labac that you suffer greatly on your way out. We looked into you. We know that you've had a love for alcohol your entire life. Well, isn't it ironic that's how you'll be going out?" The man asked.

A creep ran up my spine. That banana bag was not saline. It was vodka.

"I've set it so that you will slowly start to go through all the phases one goes through when they drink. When you're so drunk that you're about to black out, it will keep dripping until you're dead. I thought of this myself, aren't you proud of me?" The man asked.

"Screw you, you're never going to get away with this," I said.

"Oh, but I have already. My flight leaves in an hour. I must get going as soon as I hook your friend up to the same thing," the man said.

It took him a few minutes to get the IV in place, Josh wasn't cooperating very well. Finally though, it was in.

"Well gentlemen, I bid you adieu. The great famine which I sense approaching, will often turn, then become worldwide, it will be so vast and long lasting that they will grab Roots from the trees and children from the breast. Do say hi to the Pindar when you see her for me won't you?" The man said as he put his hat on and left the room.

"Graham. Are you ok?" Josh asked.

"I am, but we need to figure out how to get out of here." I said as I started to feel my arm go cold from the vodka. At least this guy had the decency to pour us a frozen shot.

"Nostradamus," Josh said.

"What?" I asked.

"That quatrain he just said. It was from Nostradamus," Josh said.

We both struggled to free ourselves, but we were strapped down. I could feel myself slowly starting to get buzzed. When alcohol goes directly in your veins, it's almost immediate. I hadn't felt this feeling in a while. I started to get very happy despite my current situation and my inhibitions were slowly fading away.

"Graham, stay with me," Josh said as I could tell he was getting woozy too. Josh then sneezed, which shook his entire body. The dentist's chair went up on one side and came back down.

"Do that again Josh," I said.

"I don't have to sneeze," he said.

"No, rock your body from side to size. I don't think your chair is as secured down as mine is," I said, starting to feel even woozier.

Josh rocked back and forth as hard as he could. At first the left side raised up just an inch, but the more he rocked it, the more it rose, until the entire thing toppled over, and he fell to the right.

"Josh, are you ok?" I asked.

"I'll be fine, just hit my head. I have a feeling when I'm sober it'll hurt a lot more. I'll be over to you in a minute," he said.

His fall loosened up a strap on his right arm, the one with the needle in it. He pulled his forearm to his mouth and ripped the needle out with his teeth. Blood shot everywhere. He then took the needle and started cutting through the strap to his left arm. After a few minutes of that, he was finally free. He took a look over at me and I wasn't doing so good.

"Graham, are you still with me?" He asked.

By this point my vision was being impaired, but I was not hammered. I was at that drunk place that everyone chances when they party, but never know when to stop so they blow past it.

"Just hurry," I said. I could tell my speech was a little slurred.

Josh woozied his way over to me, and quickly ripped the needle out of my arm. He then undid my straps after a few moments of drunken fumbling. Just like that, we were out.

"Ok, so what now?" Josh asked.

"I call the girls," I said as I pulled my shoe off and took out a miniscule phone.

"What is that?" Josh asked.

"I borrowed it from Larisa a while back. It's an emergency mini phone. Can only dial pre-programmed numbers," I said.

"Let's hope it works," Josh said as he grabbed the two needles from the floor and handed me one. Just in case someone was still here.

"Larisa, it's Graham," I said.

“Thank God you’re ok, but you don’t sound too good,” she said.

“We’re pretty drunk right now,” I said.

“What? Graham is this the time for . . .” She said as I cut her off.

“It wasn’t my choice. I’ll explain everything later. I’m in West Roxbury, can you triangulate?” I asked.

“Give me a minute. Hey Hannah, your husband is ok. They’re both drunk but ok. Yeah, I don’t know either. Graham, are you still there? I’m sending a message to Kurt to pick you up in the squad car. Nobody is going to mess with you if the police are there. Just hold on tight,” she said.

“Thanks girl,” I said as I hung up the phone. I burped and almost felt it come up. I debated whether or not to make myself throw up, but I puke pretty loudly and didn’t want anybody to hear me if they were outside the room.

“You ready to leave this place? I asked.

“Yeah, let’s go,” Josh said.

We quietly opened the door and looked outside. Took me a few seconds to focus and see straight, but it was empty. This guy really just did leave us. We made our way through the hall and to an elevator. I hit the button. The elevator came a moment later and I hit the main floor and went outside. We waited for Kurt to pick us up and after about a half an hour, he was there.

"Jesus are you two ok?" Kurt asked as he looked us up and down covered in blood.

"We'll be fine, just please get us home," I said.

"You got it," Kurt said as we got in the back of the squad car. He threw the wailers on, and we were off. We had about 46 hours before the bombs went off.

From the depths of the West of Europe, a young child will be born of poor people, he who by his tongue will seduce a great troop, his fame will increase towards the realm of the east.

Beasts ferocious with hunger will cross the rivers, the greater part of the battlefield will be against Hister, into a cage of iron will the great one be drawn, when the child of Germany observes nothing.

—*Nostradamus's quatrains predicting Hitler*

Chapter Twenty

"Well, is it done?" Labac asked through the speaker-phone.

"It is finished as it has been said," the man on the other line came through.

Labac got excited and started stamping around the room. "Tell me, what did you do to them? Did they know anything?" He asked.

"The children knew nothing, I made sure of it. I tied them down to a reclining chair and hooked an IV full of vodka to them," the man said.

"How delightful. Well, now that they are out of the way, we should probably begin our celebration," Labac said as he crushed up some methamphetamine. "Beez, hand me my pipe will you."

"Sure thing," Beez said.

"I trust there will be no more complications. Is everything still going as planned?" Labac asked.

"Everything is box tight sir. I have to go now. I'll call you when this is over," the man said.

"Were you able to retrieve the scrolls?" Labac asked.

"Negative, but none of Graham's friends know anything about it either if he doesn't. They'll be so at a loss with their friend. They'll never be able to figure it out," the man said.

"Did you physically watch them die?" Labac asked.

"I did not. The plane you had waiting for me, I would have missed it if I stayed. But trust me, I strapped them down myself, they weren't going anywhere," the man said.

"I don't like the sound of that, but that's good news," Labac said.

"I've already been on the social platforms and spread the info that Graham Newsdon is dead. It's trending now actually," the man said.

"Excellent. Well, I'll see you when you get here," Labac said as he took a hit out of his pipe and coughed it all immediately out. "Got to go."

"Everything alright sir?" Beez asked.

"No, everything is fine. It's just that when you take this poison in, you immediately have to take a dump. It's like your body is rushing it out of you. Today is a celebration," Labac said as he left the room.

Labac walked down the hallway and turned right at the corridor. He walked a few more feet until he was at the bathroom. He stayed in there for about 20 minutes just feeling the high, feeling the energy, feeling the excitement. He wouldn't sleep for three days on this, but he didn't care. By the time he came down, London would be burning so to speak. Labac finished up what he was doing and went back in the room. He caught Beez taking a hit off his pipe. Labac smiled. It was funny, they say that if you end up with one good friend when you're older you're lucky. They also say that the higher you climb, the smaller the window and the harder you fall. Labac was on top of the world, literally. The most covert leader on the planet. All great decisions for war, famine, diseases, ran through him. He thought about how Graham Newsdon had stopped their plans over and over again. Labac started to get angry, but then smiled when he realized that Graham was dead, and the world was starting to learn that fact. He looked at his watch, under two days now until the coke can size nuclear bombs they had placed would go off, obliterating everything that the World had worked so hard for. Nothing could bring him more joy than that. Well maybe one thing.

"Lock the door Beez," Labac said as he took another drag off the pipe.

"I thought you'd never ask," Beez said as he went to lock the door.

"Hold off a second," Labac said as he lifted his phone receiver and asked one of their onsite prostitutes to meet in the room. "I have a treat for you tonight Beez."

"You're bringing her into this?" He asked.

"Tonight is a special night Beez." Labac said as he dropped down and started doing pushups.

The lady walked into the room and Labac instructed her to lock the door behind her. When she turned around, they were both naked already. She smiled and walked slowly towards them, picking up the pipe and taking a long hit before meeting them in the middle of the room.

If you wish to seduce an angel, you must play the part of a devil—Eliphas Levi

Chapter Twenty-One

40 hours until explosion

Kurt dropped us off at Jean's place.

"Um, Kurt, we might need your help with something," I said.

"What is that exactly?" He asked.

"Can you just come with us please?" I pleaded, still intoxicated.

"Fine," he said and got out of the car.

We walked to the lounge and stopped by the TV for a moment when I saw my picture on it.

"This is Jennifer Polizzi reporting live that Graham Newsdon, local celebrity has died from alcohol poisoning. These rumors are not yet confirmed, yet it is spreading like wildfire all over Aquastream. More on this as it comes in."

I blinked. This must have been Labac's doing. Well, one thing is for certain, I'm glad I look different than the old picture of me they had on the tv, with a shaved face and longer hair. It might buy us some time. Actually, it was a pretty good idea that everybody thought I was dead. It'll allow us to move more secretly, I thought as I used the chair to balance myself up.

"Hey, are you people ok?" A lady's voice came from behind me.

"Yeah, why would you? Oh," I said as I looked at our bloody arms and shirts.

"Do I need to call the police?" She asked.

"Lady, I am the police, they're with me. They're helping me with something," Kurt said.

"I can't remember Jean's room," I whispered to Kurt.

"Can you tell me where Mr. Solex lives?" Kurt asked the lady.

"He's in apartment 33," she said.

"OF COURSE he's in 33," I said and laughed.

"Sir, are you sure they're ok?" She asked Kurt.

"We're just going to be a little while," Kurt said.

We walked down the hall, until we got to 33. I went to knock on the door, but the door was already opened. I could hear crying and screaming from in there.

"HELLO, is anybody home?" I asked.

"Graham? Is that you?" Hannah asked as she ran over to me and gave me an enormous hug. "I just saw the news, I thought you were dead."

"I am, let's just keep it that way for now," I said.

"Why am I here guys?" Kurt asked.

“Yeah, about that,” I said as I looked up at the chandelier and there were no more bodies hanging. “Hannah, where are the bodies?”

“Wait, what? Bodies?” Kurt asked.

“Yeah, so Graham, about 2 hours after you left some men came to the apartment and took them away and cleaned up. One of them kept a gun on us the entire time. They wouldn’t tell us their names,” Hannah said.

“Graham, what the hell have you gotten yourself into?” Kurt asked.

“Don’t worry about it, Kurt. But yeah Hannah, it must be some more of Labac’s men. I guess they need physical proof of the bodies,” I said.

“Well, what about you?” She asked.

Everybody started coming to the front. A look of shock and awe at us.

“Yes guys, we’re still alive,” I said.

“Alright, well if nobody needs me, I’m going to go,” Kurt said.

Hannah walked up to him, wiping her tears away from her face and gave him a big hug.

“I’m not used to seeing you without your Hawaiian shirt on,” Hannah said and laughed.

“We’ll get together soon. I have to go right now. Take care guys,” Kurt said as he disappeared down the hallway.

"So, Graham, what now?" Rosette asked.

"First, somebody get the scrolls. Second, Hannah please make us a barrel of coffee. I need to clear my head," I said as I went to the bathroom and unloaded the longest piss of my life.

I came back out after a minute, and Hannah had two cups of coffee for Josh and me.

"Alright guys, we have by my count," as I looked at my watch, "39 hours until the bombs are going to go off. The key has to be on these scrolls," I said as I pounded the coffee and handed Hannah the cup for a refill.

"How are you feeling Graham? I mean did they really get you that drunk? Both of you?" Rosette asked.

"They tied us down and hooked us up to IV's full of vodka," Josh said.

"Oh my God. Those sons of bitches. How did you get free?" Larisa asked.

"That's not really important right now. Let me see the scrolls," I said.

Larisa nodded and handed one of them over to me.

"OK, so this one has a map and Norway has been cut out. So, I'm guessing it has to be in Norway. But what is so important in Norway?" I asked.

"Not sure," Jackson said.

"Wait what's that?" Jean asked as he pointed to the back of the map.

"What's what?" I asked.

"Turn the map over. It looks like something was written on it, but removed," he said.

I turned the map over and looked it over.

"Hannah, can you get my magnifying glass?" I asked her.

She nodded and took off into the bedroom.

"Why do you have a magnifying glass in your bedroom? Is there something you're not sharing with us?" Jackson asked.

"Jackson, while I appreciate your humor to try and make me forget I was almost just murdered instead of saying something like 'If Isaac Newton created calculus in order to show the effects of gravity, then why is it not conceivable to think a new method of calculating the value and effect in a multidimensional entity would have on its reality as a whole, I have to tell you something. This is called a palimpsest. Old scrolls were erased to make way for new writing, but the old writing remains below. Here, hand me the glass lovebug," I said.

Hannah handed it over to me.

I looked at it for a few moments.

"What's it say?" Jean asked.

"The fire by night will take hold in two lodgings. Several within suffocated and roasted. It will happen near two rivers as one. Sun, Sagittarius and Capricorn will all be reduced," I said.

"That's another Nostradamus quatrain," Eli said.

"I had as much a feeling. Somebody write that down. Let me see the other scroll," I said to Larisa.

She handed me the smaller scroll.

> **Since the earliest of civilizations, there has always been a struggle for people to avoid catastrophes.**
>
> **Even when everything seems to be going well, civilizations have fallen to dust. If not that, then war endlessly ravages the lands. The old way of doing things is no longer applicable. This world is beyond doing anything for. We can no longer save it. Countries like the United States and Russia will always vehemently be at battle with one another. We need a global reset. We are overpopulated and it was only a matter of time before our land would sink to the bottom of the ocean like Atlantis, unless we put a stop to it now. I've left you clues within this letter that will help you locate the area lovingly chosen as the beginning of the end. It's**

time to start from scratch, see what new arises.

This was always the end game for each secret society known to man. Let's burn this motherfucker.

"Can you make anything out of that?" Jackson asked.

"It's just New World Order mumbo jumbo," Eli said.

I turned to him. "Do you have any idea how much mumbo jumbo turns out to be a hidden codex somehow. What am I missing right now? I asked everybody as I was starting to feel better from the coffee, aside from the fact that I had to piss like a donkey again.

"Wait, there's something weird about this," Jean said.

"What's that?" Larisa asked.

"Look, you see where it says 'we are overpopulated, there's a space there where they could have fit another word. The next word was and, which would have easily fit, but they didn't. They chose to put it on the next line," Jean said.

I looked at him. He doesn't usually have these kind of fire thoughts.

"That's good Jean, but what could that mean?" Hannah asked.

I can't keep looking at this scroll, it's giving me a headache. Jean, do you have a white board we can write this on?" I asked.

"I keep one always for situations like this, I'll be right back," he said as he disappeared into his bedroom.

"Yeah, I know Jackson, he's got a whiteboard in his bedroom, how can you spin that sexually?" I asked.

"Well since you called me out, I don't want to do it anymore," he said and stomped his foot like a kid, then broke out in a laugh.

Jean rolled out the whiteboard. "OK, who's got the best handwriting here?" He asked.

We all looked at him and laughed.

"Fine, I'll do it," he said.

He transcribed the entire thing again.

Since the earliest of civilizations, there has always been a struggle for people to avoid catastrophes.

Even when everything seems to be going well, civilizations have fallen to dust. If not that, then war endlessly ravages the lands. The old way of doing things is no longer applicable. This world is beyond doing anything for. We can no longer save it. Countries like the United States and Russia

will always vehemently be at battle with one another. We need a global reset. We are overpopulated and it was only a matter of time before our land would sink to the bottom of the ocean like Atlantis, unless we put a stop to it now. I've left you clues within this letter that will help you locate the area lovingly chosen as the beginning of the end. It's time to start from scratch, see what new arises.

This was always the end game for each secret society known to man. Let's burn this motherfucker.

"There's something here, I'm just not seeing it right now. Ugh, come on guys," I said. I looked at my watch again, 37 hours left. I did a quick calculation in my head. Getting to Norway would take us at least 7-8 hours. That means we actually have closer to 29 hours left.

We stared at the board for a little while. I stood up when I noticed the first sentence on each line, the capital letters spelled the word SET. I shared it with the group.

"You mean SET like Sunset?" Hannah asked.

"Like the fighter of Horus?" I asked.

"Aleister Crowley mentions that the Aeon of Horus is what we're in now. It began in 1904," Eli said.

"So we're supposed to fight an imaginary God?" Jackson asked.

"Oh my God guys. I know what it is," I said.

"What is it?" Rosette asked.

"I was looking at the capital letters at the start of each sentence, but what I didn't do was look at ALL the letters at the beginning of each sentence. It's called an acrostic. Do you see what it spells?" I asked.

"S.E.E.D.V.A.U.L.T," Larisa said.

"Oh my God. These people are going to blow up the global seed vault. If ever there was a catastrophe, we wouldn't be able to recover without it," Rosette said.

"Larisa, look it up. Where is the global seed vault?" I asked.

"Gimme a sec. Aw crap Graham," she said.

"What?" I asked.

"It's in Norway," she replied.

"Where exactly, what city?" I asked.

"It's in Svalbard. It's a northern territory of Norway, it's not technically in Norway. I mean it is in Norway," she stammered.

"Larisa!" I shouted.

"Right. So there's an airport there and the seed vault is literally only a 7-minute drive from it. How soon can we have the plane ready to go?" I asked Jean.

"Nobody will be able to do anything until morning," Jean said.

"Damn it. That brings us down to 17 hours left. Also, we have no idea what it's going to be like when we get there," Rosette said.

"Jean, make the call," I said. He nodded, took his phone out and turned around.

"Guys this is it. This is their end game. We have to be careful," I said.

"Alright guys, plane's getting ready. We leave first thing in the morning," Jean said.

We sat down and I took a quick nap. I was completely and utterly exhausted. I have no idea what they talked about while I was out cold. The last thing I remember before I dozed off was that quatrain from Nostradamus. I couldn't help but think that's how our situation was going to play out.

"He said it would take me higher than I'd ever been." —Fear and Loathing in Las Vegas talking about the human adrenaline gland

Chapter Twenty-Two

"Sir, you're not going to believe this, but there was a plane just chartered an hour ago that's going to Norway," a man said through the speaker phone.

"So what?" Labac asked.

"Sir, it's going to Svalbard," the man said.

"It's WHAT?!" Labac yelled.

"What should we do sir. Our team has already gone back to Florida," the man said.

"Where was the plane chartered from?" Labac asked.

"From Logan sir," the man said.

Labac looked at the glass he was drinking his cognac from and threw it into the fireplace. It erupted.

"I guess we're heading to Norway. Get the jet ready," Labac said to the man.

"Are you sure that's such a good idea Labac? I mean these are mini nuclear bombs we're talking about," Beez said.

"I can't risk this, there's too much at stake. All our planning, all our underground facilities are up and running. As soon as the seed vault is obliterated, we can manipulate the weather to cause another great flood on this planet," Labac said.

"So that was the end game all along?" Beez asked.

Labac sighed and stepped over to him. "The planet is too populated to survive. Those that watch us from above have not gotten involved with us, so we take that as a great sign. There's been a great awakening in this new age of Aquarius. We were going to begin to install the religion of the new age, but it's nearly impossible to do. With everything on the internet and the instant access, people would reject it. It couldn't grow organically like the previous religions we put in place. No, our best bet is to see this through. We still have our boat there, remember? We'll be long gone, and the rest of Graham's team will be dead. Please get the weapon," Labac said.

"You mean, THE weapon?" Beez asked.

"Yes," Labac said.

"Tell me again what it does. I love when you explain it to me." Beez said as he stroked Labac's hair.

"Well dear friend, the United States military invented a gun with no bullets. They were ice pellets that you fire, and inside the ice pellets there would be a shellfish toxin. The shot only leaves a red dot on the skin, the poison goes in, causes massive cardiac collapse, then disappears from the body. No way to trace it. I'm going to kill those kids. I knew I shouldn't have let them live," Labac said.

"I'll go get it and get my things ready. I'm assuming you need me on this trip?" Beez asked.

Labac grabbed his friend's hand and pulled it away from his hair. "Unfortunately old friend, I'm going to have to do this alone. Too many variables. It's been a long time since I've been in the field, but the times are calling for it," Labac said.

"Are you sure?" Beez asked.

Labac nodded.

"I'll go get the gun, you get ready, and I'll drive you to the plane," Beez said.

"What's my ETA? Labac asked.

"Well, we're still in California and it's a 2 hour drive to the airport. Then the flight is going to be about 12 hours long. You should still have time before it goes off," Beez replied.

"Thank you, old friend. Please hurry," Labac said.

Beez bowed and left the room. Labac took the bottle of cognac and cradled it in his hand. He thought to take a nice swig directly from the bottle, but he figured he would save it for when he got back. If all went as planned, in 48 hours he would have his cognac. He would also commission the greatest orgy ever seen on the premises of Germany. Beez came back in the room with the gun and handed it to Labac.

"One now and one for the road?" Beez asked.

"What do you mean?" Labac asked.

Beez smiled and pulled a syringe from behind his back as well as two vials. The vials were dark red and Labac knew exactly what he was talking about.

"You're too good to me," Labac said as he took his coat and tie off and used his tie to make a tourniquet. Beez smiled as he injected a vial of that sweet magic juice.

All at once Labac was reenergized and full of life. There's nothing better than fresh child's blood to reinvigorate you. Labac put his tie and coat jacket back on and nodded his head. They walked down the hallway and Labac made a sharp right and opened the second door.

"Give me a moment will you, old friend?" Beez asked.

"Not a problem," Beez said.

Labac walked into the room and shut the door. This is where they were keeping the bodies of Amrita and his daughter. He walked up to Amrita and smiled and shook his head. Then, he walked over to his daughter who was stiff as a board and frozen cold and planted a kiss on her forehead. He then turned around and walked out of the room. They walked downstairs to the parking garage and got in a Bentley. Tomorrow Labac was going to end the legacy of Graham Newsdon.

"Stupidity is the top of the list for Satanic sins. The Cardinal Sin of Satanism. It's too bad that stupidity isn't painful. Ignorance is one thing, but our society thrives increasingly on stupidity. It depends on people going along with whatever they are told. The media promotes a cultivated stupidity as a posture that is not only acceptable but laudable. Satanists must learn to see through the tricks and cannot afford to be stupid"—Anton LaVey

Chapter Twenty-Three

16 hours left

We were about an hour out from the Svalbard airport.

"Hey guys do you want to hear a great story?" I asked.

Everybody stopped what they were doing. Jackson took his EarPods off.

"So, the first time I ever met Hannah's extended family, her Godfather basically, he had us over to his house. Now he's real old school Italian. You wouldn't think this, but Hannah does have Italian in her. So basically for a few weeks she's prepping me. What fork goes to what, what spoon goes to where that sort of thing. Actually, a funny side story, the Catholic Church used to ban the use of forks. Saint Pier Damiani called it a demonic object.

They used to eat with their bare hands. They considered this a tool of the devil," I said as I was interrupted.

"Finish the story already," Rosette said.

"Alright, so she's prepping me and after a few weeks I'm starting to get the hang of it. Finally, the big day comes. We go to an Italian bakery and pick up fresh pastries and go to the house. Oh my God. The amount of food this man cooked was insane. We had seafood first. At one point he told me to slow down. That I wasn't going to be ready for the other courses. Yes, there are other courses, and they are taken very seriously. He's filling me up with homemade Limoncello and telling stories about Hannah and her family. I start to get a little tipsy. He goes into the kitchen and brings back some broccoli rabe. Now, I hate broccoli rabe, I find it to be too bitter. So, he tries to give me some, and I shake my head. He goes 'What, you no a like broccoli rabe?' So me like a dumbass and slightly tipsy decide to try my Italian out." I said as Hannah started to giggle. "So, I said, 'No that's not my type of vegetable, I'd much rather have finocchio.' I turned around and the entire table went silent, and Hannah turned beet red."

"What? So you asked for some fennel. What's the big deal about that?" Jackson asked.

"Because little did I know that finocchio in Italian where he's from in Italy means fennel, but it was more commonly used to describe a flamboyant gay man," I said.

The entire plane burst out in laughter. Including the pilots.

"So wait. You're a new boyfriend, you meet the family and you said that you'd much rather prefer a gay man for dinner?" Larisa asked.

Hannah burst out laughing.

"The best part was after what felt like a million years, my Godfather just burst out laughing. When he did, the whole table did as well. It was probably the most embarrassing thing that could ever have happened at that dinner. Anyway, they kept feeding him Limoncello and at the end he went in the TV room with my cousins and watched wrestling," Hannah said.

"You're still into wrestling?" Rosette asked.

"I did it for them!" I pleaded.

"Sure you did finocchio. They were testing you to see if you were getting excited off the spandex," Rosette said.

Hannah laughed and walked up to Rosette and gave her a kiss on the head.

Just then our plane started to make its descent. Surprisingly though, my ears didn't pop this time around.

We landed and Jean had called ahead and set us up with a vehicle. It wasn't the greatest looking one, but it was big enough for all of us. Larisa jumped out of the plane with her backpack on, no doubt holding on to some hacking equipment if we needed it.

"Alright guys, do we know where we're going?" Jackson asked.

"We'll follow the GPS. It says it's only about a 10-minute ride or so," Jean said as he got in the driver's seat. I'm not sure at what point Jean became the official taxi, but I was loving it.

We drove very slowly as there was much ice everywhere. After getting lost shortly, we were back on track, and we made it to the site. There were three people outside of it, armed, looking around. We backed the car up until we were out of sight.

"Guys what are we going to do about them? Also, we don't know exactly where we're going to find these and even more than that, how are we going to diffuse or get rid of them," Josh said.

"Thanks for pointing out the obvious. Actually, that's a really good point. Did any of you bring the scroll?" I asked.

Although squeezed tightly in the back together, Eli handed it to me. I unraveled it.

"There's nothing on this map that shows anything," I said.

"Well, we obviously can't go in now that it's light out. Also, I could take maybe one, maybe two of them, but three of them all armed, no way," Jackson said.

"Well, that's not going to be a problem," Larisa said as she reached into her bag and pulled out a gun.

"You brought this with you?" I asked.

"Yeah, well I had to. As a precaution," she said.

"Well, nobody here knows how to fire one of these," I said.

Jackson stirred.

"I do, Graham. Don't you remember the beach?" He said.

"Oh. That's true. So, wait, you're just going to go in and waste these people?" I asked.

"I think we should try and talk to them first," Rosette said.

"And tell them what exactly?" I asked.

"What we know," Eli said.

"We don't know where the bombs are. How do you think that's going to play out?" I asked.

"The fire by night will take hold in two lodgings. Several within suffocated and roasted. It will happen near two rivers as one. Sun, Sagittarius and Capricorn will all be reduced," Josh said.

"What are you getting at?" I asked.

"We're waiting until nighttime. The fire by night. Several within suffocated and roasted. You want to kill these guards. It will happen near two rivers as one. Not rivers, but we are where the Arctic and Atlantic Oceans meet. Sun, Sagittarius and Capricorn will all be reduced. We're in the Age of Aquarius right now. If this bomb goes off and a pandemic hits, the people that will survive the Age of Aquarius and after that, Capricorn, and after that, Sagittarius will be reduced because we won't be able to repopulate. This would send us back to the stone age," Josh said.

"Oh my God," Hannah said.

"Come on. What are the chances that Nostradamus predicted this? Does it really have to end the way he said it does?" Jean said.

"It's pretty damn close if you think of it," Rosette said.

"Alright then answer this. He says two lodgings. We're at one location. Does that mean that there is another location that we don't know about?" Jean asked.

We were all silent.

"I have no idea Jean, but I do think we should wait until night and then approach the guard and try and reason with them," Larisa said.

"Fine," Jackson said.

We waited calmly for 12 hours for the Sun to go down. Finally, as we were about to fall asleep, it began to set. We didn't know if this was going to go in our favor or not, so we decided to send myself as well as Rosette with a gun. We were going to send Jackson, but we thought that he might be too big and intimidating for our liking.

4 hours until explosion

Rosette and I walked over to the guards.

"Stop right there. Who are you?" The first guard answered.

"Listen very carefully. My name is Graham Newsdon, and there is a bomb in your facility," I said.

The guards looked over at one another.

"Make that two bombs," I said, shaking my head that I didn't say that originally.

"Bull. This place is on lockdown 24/7. Anything going on in here we would know it. We have top of the line security system and computer monitoring. We would know if something was up," the second man said.

"Listen gentlemen," I said, "We only have about," I started as I looked at my watch, "three hours left, to get two bombs out of your facility and out of here," I said.

"OK smartass. So, where are they?" The third man asked.

I felt defeated. “I have no idea, but I know they are in there, that’s for sure,” I said.

“Yeah ok, step back,” the first man said.

I stepped back slowly and started to walk away.

“Wait, did you say your name was Graham Newsdon?” The second man asked me.

I turned around “I did,” I said.

“Ha! Graham Newsdon is dead. I just read about it online a day ago,” the third man said.

I walked directly to them and looked them all in the eye. “Listen up. I’m Graham Newsdon. I survived and I’m standing in front of you right now. I have a beard now and I shaved my head. Go ahead, ask me anything,” I said.

“Wait here just a minute,” the third man said as he walked back inside.

We waited outside guns trained on us for a few minutes, until that man came back out. Finally, we saw him out of the shadows.

“Tell me about the 144,000,” The third man said as he was scrolling through his phone.

“What do you mean?” I asked.

“The Mormons say that only 144,000 people can enter Heaven. I want to know where that comes from,” the man said.

I turned to Rosette and frowned. I didn't know it was going to come to this, so close to the bomb blast, but I was going to have to give them something.

"The number 144,000 isn't by accident. It has nothing to do with Astrology. What it has to do with is the Chakras in the human body. See, Christ consciousness gets you to the top Chakra which is where everybody wants to go. Jacob's ladder is a metaphor for the 33 vertebrae the sacred oil or Christ needs to climb to enter the Pineal Gland and explode into all that is knowing. The religions of the world want to keep you on lower chakras, which they do," I said.

They looked at each other.

"What about the 144,000?" The third man asked again, this time drawing his gun at me.

"Ok ok. The root chakra has 4 petals. The sacral has 6. The solar plexus has 10. The heart has 12 and the throat has 16, which equals 48. The third eye chakra, or the pineal gland represents 96 and only has 2 petals because it is two times as powerful as the five lower chakras. The Crown chakra is 1000 times more powerful than the lower 6 chakras. When you add the lower 6 you get 144 and when you multiply it by the top chakra, 1000, you get 144,000," I said as I exasperated on my breath.

The men looked at each other. The third man looked at his phone and held it up to me. Looked at the phone, then looked at me.

"You are Graham Newsdon!" The third man said.

"How did you survive?" The second man asked.

"Look, I'll explain everything later, but we don't have much time. We have about 3 hours left until the bombs go off. Now can we please come inside?" I asked.

The men looked at each other and lowered their guns. I breathed a sigh of relief. I turned to our car behind me and waved them over. I turned to Rosette and motioned her to put her gun away. We were about to head inside with 2 hours and 50 minutes before a nuclear explosion rocked the area, and we had not a clue where the bombs were hidden.

When you're taught to love everyone, to love your enemies, then what value does that place on love?
—Marilyn Manson

Chapter Twenty-Four

2.5 hours left

Everyone got out of the car and started walking to us slowly. Finally, they made their way to us.

"Jesus Christ, look at the size of this guy," the first man said.

"Relax, I'm harmless. I'm more of a lover rather than a fighter," Jackson said.

"Whatever you say big man," the second man said.

They turned around and we walked inside. We walked down a long corridor.

"Do you guys have any idea where these bombs would be?" The third man asked.

"We don't know," Larisa said.

"Alright, so we'll sweep every room," the first man said as he brought us into the first room.

1 hour 56 minutes left

Nothing in the first room. We went to the next room. This room had a bunch of servers in them. Although it would be orgasmic for Larisa to rip through all of these, we canvassed the entire room, and unfortunately found nothing. We went to the third room.

"How many rooms are there?" I asked.

"Six, if you include the two seed rooms," the second man said.

"Wait, what do you mean two seed rooms?" Jackson asked.

"We have seeds from every country on this planet in the event of a catastrophe. There's 196 countries on Earth right now and that's too many plastic bins for just one room, so we split it into two," the first man said.

Damn it. We were going to have to go through each and every bin. That was going to take more time than we had left.

1 hour and 11 minutes left

We finished the third room. To save time, we split up in two groups. We met outside the rooms at roughly the same time.

"Anything?" I asked.

"No," Rosette said as she hugged Jackson.

It began to occur to us that we might not survive today. I couldn't help but think back to the message that not all of us would survive. Does that mean that only some of us would survive, or that none of us would? This question tortured me.

55 minutes until explosion

We walked into the fifth room. This room was wall to wall covered in bins with the country's name on a label on the front of the bin.

"Guys," I began trying to spill the awful truth, "There's a decent chance that we're not going to make it out of here," I said.

"What do you mean baby?" Hannah asked.

"We have 53 minutes until the bombs go off. We can't possibly go through two rooms of bins. Inside one of these bins are two bombs that are set to go off," I said.

I turned to the guards. "I suggest you guys get the hell out of here. No need in risking your lives," I said.

"We're here to protect this place, if you're here, then we're here," the first man said.

I nodded at him and put my fist to my heart.

"Does anybody have any idea where they might be?" Rosette asked.

"Are all these bins alphabetically?" Larisa asked.

The men nodded.

"Maybe if I can hack into those computers in the other room, it could buy us more time," she said.

I turned to her and shot her an angry face.

"This isn't the time Larisa," I said.

"But it could help," she replied.

“No, it can’t we have 47 minutes until the bombs go off,” I said.

“Wait, what about the other scroll?” Josh asked.

“What about it?” I asked.

“Wasn’t there a message on the back of it? Could it help?” Eli asked.

I thought back to the other scroll and then it struck me.

“Jackson, you’re the fastest. Go back to the car and bring me back the scroll,” I said.

Jackson saluted and turned around and took off.

39 minutes until explosion

Jackson came back into the room completely out of breath. I could tell he ran faster than he ever did in his entire life. I took the scroll from him, then reached into my pocket and lit up a cigarette.

> **Since the earliest of civilizations, there has always been a struggle for people to avoid catastrophes.**
>
> **Even when everything seems to be going well, civilizations have fallen to dust. If not that, then war endlessly ravages the lands. The old way of doing things is no longer applicable. This world is beyond doing any-**

thing for. We can no longer save it. Countries like the United States and Russia will always vehemently be at battle with one another. We need a global reset. We are overpopulated and it was only a matter of time before our land would sink to the bottom of the ocean like Atlantis, unless we put a stop to it now. I've left you clues within this letter that will help you locate the area lovingly chosen as the beginning of the end. It's time to start from scratch, see what new arises.

This was always the end game for each secret society known to man. Let's burn this motherfucker.

"Where did you get that from?" The first man asked.

"It doesn't matter. What matters is that the bombs have to be in the United States and Russian bin. Jackson, go open them up and grab them," I said.

The first man drew his gun and aimed it at Jackson.

"I wouldn't do that if I were you," he said.

My heart sank. This entire time, they had a man on the inside.

"What are you doing?" The second man asked.

"Shut up. I can't believe how far you've gotten with all of this, but this has gone too far," the first man said.

“Listen to me, countless people are going to die because of this. You have to let us get the bombs out of here and out into the water,” I said.

The first man laughed. “Do you have any idea how dumb you sound right now. We need to set the seeds in motion. HA! Do you see what I did there with the word seeds?” The first man said.

The other two men looked at him. They had left their guns at the front as they were supposed to when then entered the building. The first man did not share the same sentiment.

“Now, it was only going to be us three that died here tonight, but since you’ve been so burdensome, we’ll all wait here together. We have 31 minutes left. So, let’s see. What do you all want to talk about?” The first man asked.

Just then the third man leapt across and started struggling with the first man. They went back and forth, the gun was the focal point of their struggle. All of a sudden, we heard a gunshot and we all leapt back. The third man grabbed his stomach and fell back to the ground.

“Right, so anybody else have any bright ideas?” He asked.

We sat there in silence.

"Good," he said. "25 minutes left. Can't you feel the power of the World about to change? The first man asked.

"I am not going to sit here and die with you, you crazy son of a bitch, the second man said as he leapt for the first man. The first man raised his gun in the air and caught the third man with a bullet in the head. It stopped his forward progress immediately, and he fell down like a sack of potatoes.

Just then we heard another gunshot. I looked around to see where it came from and stared at the first man. He grabbed his chest and tried to raise his gun in the air to shoot at us. When the gun was at chest height, he started to struggle and fell to the ground, dead.

I looked around and didn't see anything. I turned around and saw Rosette holding the gun that Larisa brought in between her hands. Her hands were shaking terribly, and Jackson walked over to her slowly with his hands up and carefully removed it from her hands.

"You ok Rose?" I asked.

"I've never shot anybody before," she said.

"Baby, we'll get through this," Jackson said.

"Just get that gun away from me," she replied.

"OK, OK," Jackson said as he handed it off to Josh.

"Lucky for us U and R are near each other, can you bring the bins down from up there?" I asked pointing to the top.

"Right away," Jackson said.

It took him a minute or two to get up there and turn and drop the bins at us. Eli and I caught both of them. Now was the moment of truth. We opened the bins.

Chapter Twenty-Five

20 minutes until explosion

We opened up the bins. There were two soda bottle sized bombs in there with a countdown of 20 minutes.

"Guys, we need to get out of here now!" Jean screamed.

"Where are we going with these?" Rosette asked.

"To the airplane?" Larisa asked.

"By the time we get there, and it takes off, we'll have run out of time. Not to mention that we'll have killed the pilot," I said.

"There's got to be something that we can do," Hannah said.

"To the water," I said off the cusp.

"What do you mean?" Jackson asked.

"We need to get to the car and drive to the water," I said.

"OK guys, I'll see you at the car," Jackson said as he turned around running.

I picked the two bombs up and started hauling ass to the car. It took about two or three minutes, but we got to the car together. I was completely out of breath. Damn cigarettes.

"Jean, hit the gas," Larisa said as we squeezed into the car.

Jean floored it and followed the directions. What should have taken us 10 minutes took us 8.

12 minutes to explosion

We parked by the water and were surprised to see two boats there. We got out of the car and ran up to the first one. Just as we got there, a familiar face came out of the cabin.

"Graham Newsdon I presume," Labac said. "Step back everyone."

"Labac Hamashiach Morgenstern," Eli said.

"Very good. You know who I am. What I can't figure out is how you got this far. I'll admit, seeing you running towards me, Graham, I had no idea that you were still alive. Apparently, my people can't do anything right. Well, no matter. We're all going to sit here and wait," he said.

I took a few steps forward. He pulled a gun on me.

"Now now, don't make any stupid moves. You don't know what this gun is or what it can do. I was initially going to make sure the bombs went off, but when I saw your plane land I thought, why don't we all die together," Labac said.

"Please, you don't know what you're doing. Countless people are going to suffer because of you," I said.

"Oh yes, countless," he said as he closed his eyes.

"What's he doing?" Jackson asked me.

I shook my head not knowing.

"O Master of sublime name and great power, supreme Master; O Master Saturn: Thou, the Cold, the Sterile, the Mournful, the Pernicious; Thou, whose life is sincere and whose words sure: Thou, the Sage and Solitary, the Impenetrable; Thou, whose promises are kept; Thou who art weak and weary; Thou who hast cares greater than any other, who knowest neither pleasure nor joy; Thou, the old and cunning, master of all artifice, deceitful, wise, and judicious; Thou who bringest prosperity or ruin, and makest men to be happy or unhappy! I conjure thee, O Supreme Father, by Thy great benevolence and thy generous bounty, to do for me what I ask," he said as he started to shake.

"Damn it," Eli said.

"What?" I asked.

"That's from the Picatrix, he just summoned Saturn, the Ancient God that is the beginning of all that is religion," Eli said.

"So what?" I asked.

"It's an incantation. He's making his final stand," Eli said.

I turned to Labac and he slowly opened his eyes. They were fire orange.

"Your time is over Graham Newsdon," he said as he pointed the gun at me.

"No!" Josh yelled as he pulled the gun out of his pocket and fired three rounds into Labac. Labac stunned, fell back into the boat.

I eased my way to the boat and looked at him. He survived the shots to his stomach and chest.

"He's still alive," I said.

"91 million people die every year throughout the world Graham. We're just speeding things up a little," Labac said.

I stepped back a few feet. Just then Larisa reached into her bag and pulled out that jar that I was busting her balls about on the plane and launched it into the boat. The ship exploded into a fireball which extended into the water. The water was on fire.

"What the hell was that?" I asked.

"That," Larisa began, "Was what I had in that jar on the plane. It's called Greek Fire," she said.

"You had Greek Fire in your possession. How did you even get that?" I asked as I looked at the boat encased in flames.

"We found a way to recreate it. Don't worry about it. What are we going to do now?" She asked.

I looked at everyone and then at the bombs. We had 5 minutes left until explosion. I picked the two bombs up and threw it in the other boat. I jumped in and turned the key. The boat roared to life. Just as I was about to throw it into gear, I felt a slam on the back of my head, then felt a push, which threw me into the water. There was fire on the water all around me.

"What are you doing?" I asked as I screamed at Josh.

"I'm sorry Graham, but I cannot let you sacrifice your life for this," Josh said.

"Why? I don't understand," I said.

Josh looked back at me then at the group. "You have a life with Hannah that you're going to build. You're going to get back to the states and tell everyone what we went through, what the elite's put us through. I on the other hand have led a life of selfishness. This is the first thing that I'm truly happy about," Josh said.

"Josh, you can't. There's got to be another way," I said as I inched towards the boat and tried to pull myself in.

"I'm sorry Graham, but I have one bullet left in this gun. Please don't make me disable you," Josh said as he aimed the gun at me.

I looked at him in the eyes and I could see his soul. I could see everything he had ever done and how this meant more to him than anything he had ever done.

“I’m T minus 3 minutes 30 seconds, Graham. I’m sorry,” Josh said.

I looked at him and realized it was a lost cause. “I love you buddy,” I said to him.

“John 15:13 Graham. ‘Greater love hath no man than this, that a man lay down his life for his friends,’ ” he said as he threw the boat into gear and launched me off the side of it.

We watched Josh disappear into a smaller and smaller dot. I turned to everyone, feeling helpless.

All of a sudden there was a great explosion, one that I had never seen before. A duel overlapping mushroom cloud deep in the ocean. We were finally safe.

“I’m sorry Graham,” Eli said.

Before I could say anything, a giant wave started making its way towards us.

“RUN!” I yelled as we booked it for the seed vault. That would be the only safe place for us to ride this out.

We ran for a few minutes as the wave came crashing. Just as it was about to hit us, we turned into the vault and down the hallway. We watched the water pass the vault and keep going.

After about 20 minutes, the water subsided, and we looked at each other.

“I guess it’s time for us to go home gang,” I said.

“I’m hella fine with that,” Rosette said.

"Me too," Hannah said.

We started walking to the car. The water was still at tire level, but the car was fine. Jean started the engine and took us back to the airport.

We cannot teach people anything; we can only help them discover it within themselves—Galileo Galilei

Chapter Twenty-Six

1 year later

"Rosette once told me that all types of evil behavior can be classified into four groups. Machiavellianism, sadism, psychopathy, and narcissism. I had struggled trying to figure out which type Labac was not. At the end I decided it didn't matter. Maybe all of them, I thought.

As I lay there with Hannah on our newly installed hammock on our balcony, I kept thinking how lucky I was. My podcast that exposed Labac and his criminal enterprise went viral, to the point where after a short time the Consortium was disbanded. Each state nation relegated to themselves again. A moratorium on all wars was declared as governments began to get to the bottom of things. The things that I've known forever but have not made much of a splash until word that we saved the global seed vault became known public. I had been on a few tv shows explaining what had happened. Sure, there was a large number of people that didn't believe what I had to say, many had preconceived notions about what or who I was to begin with. The point that mattered was that the World began to heal. Most countries began to adopt our homeless population solution and began to follow suit.

I thought back to the beginning where I was told that we needed to save the starseeds. I laughed, because not only was it the younger people that were going to lead us to a new beginning, but we had to save the seeds as well.

I took a drag of my THC pen. I had quit cigarettes and hadn't had any alcohol since that unfortunate scenario. The THC really helped with my anxiety. I used to smoke some Indica that I would get from the local legal dispensaries, but Hannah had decided that we needed to get a dog. So we did. This dog unfortunately turned out to be a TSA rescue, and every time I smoked up, it would bark at me and try and bite my ballsagna off. So I switched to the pen, and we haven't been happier since.

I laid there with my wife holding her tight. Our war was finally over. The Big Heaven Room was raided, and cadaver dogs were brought in. They found the bodies of a few children, which was enough to shut the whole thing down. I smiled as I took another hit of my THC pen. The good thing about this was that it's impossible to overdose on Marijuana because the receptors unlike opioid receptors aren't located in the brain stem in areas controlling respiration. I turned to Hannah and smiled.

Just then we heard a scream in our house that was deafening. Hannah and I looked at each other, chills ran down both our spines. Then they turned to smiles.

"I think it's your turn to get him," I said.

"No, but I'm so comfortable. Isn't it your turn?" Hannah asked.

"Pretty sure it's your turn lovebug," I said.

"Please. I didn't get much sleep last night," she said.

"Alright, I'll go in and get him," I said.

I walked back to the nursery and picked up our six-month-old baby boy. James Pierce Newsdon. After my brother and NP. We named him that on day 49 of her pregnancy. Why? Because at day 49 the soul enters the body through the pineal gland. It's the day when the pineal becomes visible and it's also the day in which the soul takes to reincarnate according to the Tibetan Book of the Dead. I cradled him in my arms until he fell back asleep after about a half an hour. I put him in his bassinet and walked back outside.

"Do you think they'll ever fully appreciate what we've done for them?" Hannah asked.

"I don't know," I began as I hit my pen again, "But I'll tell you this for damn sure. Things are about to change around here," I said.

Hannah rested her shoulder in my chest as we slowly drifted off to sleep together. After about 15 minutes, we were both on the verge of passing out. Then suddenly, everything went dark.

Coming Soon!

Into the Rabbit Hole
The Unbegun
By Micah T. Dank

The Unbegun, Book Seven, the continuation of *Into the Rabbit Hole*: 5 years later: A murder at the Kaaba in Mecca, two thieves and the purest gold that was ever created leads to the worlds markets being destroyed. A bomb waits in waiting to cover the world in ash while the elites make their way to the underground cities they've created for just this moment. Against his better judgment Graham who is fully involved as a religious commentator and has a 5-year-old son is dragged back into murder, mystery and one last chance to save the world.

www.ingramcontent.com/pod-product-compliance
Lightning Source LLC
Chambersburg PA
CBHW031830090426
42741CB00005B/193

9781645405276